NEW VANGUARD 312

# TANKS IN THE BATTLE OF GERMANY 1945

Eastern Front

STEVEN J. ZALOGA      ILLUSTRATED BY FELIPE RODRÍGUEZ

OSPREY PUBLISHING

Bloomsbury Publishing Plc

Kemp House, Chawley Park, Cumnor Hill, Oxford OX2 9PH, UK

29 Earlsfort Terrace, Dublin 2, Ireland

1385 Broadway, 5th Floor, New York, NY 10018, USA

E-mail: info@ospreypublishing.com

**www.ospreypublishing.com**

OSPREY is a trademark of Osprey Publishing Ltd

First published in Great Britain in 2022

© Osprey Publishing Ltd, 2022

A catalog record for this book is available from the British Library.

ISBN: PB 9781472848710; eBook: 9781472848703;
ePDF 9781472848734; XML: 9781472848727

22 23 24 25 26 10 9 8 7 6 5 4 3 2 1

Index by Angela Hall
Typeset by PDQ Digital Media Solutions, Bungay, UK
Printed and bound in India by Replika Press Private Ltd.

To find out more about our authors and books visit
**www.ospreypublishing.com**. Here you will find extracts, author interviews, details of forthcoming events and the option to sign up for our newsletter.

## AUTHOR'S NOTE

The Wehrmacht in World War II often designated its large-caliber guns in centimeters, but in this book all gun calibers are expressed in the more common form of millimeters; hence 75mm gun rather than 7.5cm gun.

## GLOSSARY

| | |
|---|---|
| *Abteilung* | German battalion |
| AFV | Armored Fighting Vehicle |
| DR | *Das Reich* (2.SS-Panzer-Div.) |
| FH | *Feldherrnhalle:* honorific title of some *Heer* units |
| Front | Soviet equivalent of *Heeresgruppe* or Army Group |
| GD | *Grossdeutschland* (Greater Germany) unit designation |
| *Heer* | Army |
| *Heeresgruppe* | Army Group, a German formation of several armies |
| HG | *Heeresgruppe*: Army Group, formation of several corps |
| HG | *Hermann Göring*; designation of some *Luftwaffe* field units |
| HJ | *Hitlerjugend* (12.SS-Panzer-Div.) |
| HVAP | High-Velocity Armor Piercing (projectile) |
| KStN | *Kriegsstärkenachweisungen:* War establishment strength |
| LSSAH | *Leibstandarte SS Adolf Hitler* (1.SS-Panzer-Div.) |
| OKH | *Oberkommando des Heeres*: Army High Command |
| *Panzerjäger* | Tank destroyer |
| s.Pz.Abt. | *schwere Panzer Abteilung*: Heavy tank battalion |
| s.Pz.Jg.Abt. | *schwere Panzerjäger Abteilung*: Heavy tank destroyer battalion |
| *Sturmgeschütz* | Assault gun |
| SU | *Samokhodnaya ustanovka*: Self-propelled weapon |
| Tonnes | Metric ton (1,000kg; 2,200lb) |
| *Wehrmacht* | (German) armed forces |

# CONTENTS

# TANKS IN THE BATTLE OF GERMANY 1945

## Eastern Front

### INTRODUCTION

The final battle for Germany in 1945 pitted a declining Wehrmacht against foes attacking from both east and west. This is the second book of a two-part series and covers the Russian Front; the first book covered the Western Front. This book surveys the principal tank types on both sides, as well as tank surrogates such as the tank destroyer/*Panzerjäger* and the assault gun/*Sturmgeschütz*. Due to space limitations, it does not cover self-propelled artillery or light armored vehicles such as armored cars and halftracks. For convenience's sake, the term "AFV" (Armored Fighting Vehicle) in this book refers to the tank surrogates such as assault guns and tank destroyers.

### THE CAMPAIGN

The Wehrmacht had suffered its worst defeat of the war in the summer of 1944. This started with the defeat of Heeresgruppe Mitte by the Red Army's Operation *Bagration*, which began on June 22, 1944. This allowed the Red Army to surge forward past the 1941 Soviet borders and into Poland. This offensive was finally halted to the east of Warsaw in August 1944 by the IV.SS.Panzer-Korps' counterattack. In the wake of this setback, the Red Army paused its offensive operations on the main route to Berlin. This decision was informed by three considerations. To begin with, the Red Army had exceeded its logistical support along the Berlin axis and needed to re-establish its supplies and replacements before proceeding. Secondly, its spearheads on the Berlin axis faced significant threats to their flanks, particularly from German holdouts along the Baltic coast in Kurland and East Prussia. Rather than risk a strategic envelopment of the spearheads, the Red Army began steps to clear out the German forces along the Baltic. Finally, Stalin wished to exploit the German defeats by pushing into the Balkans. While the Berlin front remained inactive after August 1944, the Red Army knocked Romania and Bulgaria out of the war, and advanced into Hungary, Slovakia, and Yugoslavia through the autumn and winter of 1944.

#### The Budapest Cauldron

At the beginning of January 1945, the most active sector of the Russian Front was centered around Budapest. Hitler was adamant that Hungary had to be

This Panther Ausf A along with about three dozen other German AFVs became bogged down and abandoned near Bieleckie-Młyny on the icy Czarna Nida River on January 17, 1945, during the massive tank battles between the Soviet 4th Tank Army and XXIV.Panzer-Korps south of Kielce, Poland. This tank, from either the 16. or 17.Panzer-Division, was severely damaged and sank in the river. It was recovered in 1990 and restored by Jacques Littlefield for his California tank museum at a cost of more than $2 million. It is seen here at its new home in the American Heritage Museum in Massachusetts in 2019.

held at all costs. Not only was Hungary one of the few remaining sources of oil due to the loss of the Romanian fields in August 1944, but it also shielded Soviet access to the oil refineries around Vienna, the Reich's other significant source of fuel.

On January 10, 1945, the Wehrmacht had 939 Panzers and AFVs in Hungary, including about 90 Tigers with the s.Pz.Abt.503 and s.Pz. bt.509. On January 1, the IV.SS-Panzer-Korps staged Operation *Konrad* in an attempt to regain control of besieged Budapest from the 3rd Ukrainian Front. Although some gains were made, the Soviet siege managed to force the surrender of the Budapest garrison on February 13.

Besides the extensive use of Wehrmacht Panzer units in the Hungarian battles, Germany's last major ally, Hungary, deployed most of its surviving tank force during the struggle for Budapest.

A pair of IS-2m heavy tanks of the 30th Guards Tank Regiment, 2nd Guards Mechanized Corps of the 2nd Ukrainian Front during the early phase of the Budapest operation in December 1944.

| Major armored formations of the 3rd Ukrainian Front near Budapest, January 1, 1945 | | | | | | |
|---|---|---|---|---|---|---|
| | T-34 | M4A2 | IS | SU-76 | SU-85 | SU-100 |
| 18th Tank Corps | 100 | | 19 | | 11 | |
| 1st Guards Mech Corps | | 184 | | | | 62 |
| 2nd Guards Mech Corps | 35 | | 8 | | 11 | |
| 7th Mech Corps | | | 65 | 12 | 14 | 10 |
| **Total** | **135** | **184** | **92** | **12** | **36** | **72** |

## The Red Army's January 1945 offensive

The Red Army renewed its offensive operations along the Berlin axis on January 12, 1945, with three simultaneous operations, the Vistula–Oder, Western Carpathian, and East Prussian strategic offensives. The Vistula–Oder offensive involved Georgi Zhukov's 1st Belorussian Front and Ivan Konev's 1st Ukrainian Front, including five mechanized corps, eight tank corps, seven independent tank brigades, five independent assault gun brigades, and numerous smaller tank and assault gun units. These formations included about 7,000 tanks and assault guns, which faced about 1,200 German Panzers, assault guns, and tank destroyers. Besides the substantial disparity in overall armored vehicle strength, the German Panzer force was severely debilitated by widespread fuel shortages caused by the Oil Campaign being waged by the US Strategic Air Forces and RAF Bomber Command over the previous several months.

One of the largest tank-vs-tank battles erupted in the Kielce area between the 4th Guards Tank Army and the XXIV.Panzer-Korps in the third week of January, involving over a thousand tanks and AFVs. By February 3, 1945, the Red Army had advanced 350 miles (565km), putting the two fronts only 40 miles (65km) from Berlin. German losses were staggering, with 35 divisions destroyed, 25 more being combat ineffective, and casualties of about a half-million men.

| Tank and AFV strength, 1st Belorussian Front, January 14, 1945 | | | | | | | |
|---|---|---|---|---|---|---|---|
| | IS-2 | T-34 | Lend-Lease tanks | SU-57 | SU-76M, SU-85 | Heavy ISU | Total |
| 1st Guards Tank Army | 42 | 511 | 0 | 94 | 85 | 21 | 753 |
| 2nd Guards Tank Army | 42 | 432 | 195 | 15 | 130 | 42 | 856 |
| Other Front Units | 176 | 778 | 87 | 23 | 843 | 144 | 2,051 |
| **Total** | **260** | **1,721** | **282** | **132** | **1,058** | **207** | **3,660** |

In the midst of a snowstorm, a column of SU-76Ms advances towards Danzig during the January 1945 East Prussia offensive. To the right is a T-34 medium tank.

While it might seem that the Red Army was poised for an immediate attack on Berlin in early February, Stalin decided against such an offensive. Konev and Zhukov's forces still had substantial German formations on their flanks along the Baltic, and there was a moderate risk of a German envelopment of the Soviet spearheads. However, in the broader strategic scheme, Stalin decided to ensure Soviet control in central Europe by continuing attacks on either side of the Vistula–Oder offensive to secure possession of Hungary, Austria, and Czechoslovakia.

The Panther Ausf G of the Festung Posen Panzer reserve, knocked out on Horst Wesel Platz on January 27, 1945, near the Church of Mary the Queen during a short duel with an IS-2M of the 34th Guards Heavy Tank Regiment.

The second Soviet offensive that began on January 12 was the Western Carpathian operation conducted by the 2nd and 4th Ukrainian Fronts, supported by two Romanian field armies. The northern portion of the offensive pushed through the Dukla Pass into southern Poland in the sector held by Heeresgruppe A. The southern wing of the attack advanced against Heeresgruppe Süd in southwestern Czechoslovakia and northwestern Hungary. In view of the difficult terrain in this sector, the offensive did not involve as large a tank force as the main offensive to the north, involving a total of one tank corps and two mechanized corps, both with the 2nd Ukrainian Front to the south of the Carpathian Mountains. The 2nd Ukrainian Front also reinforced the continuing efforts of the 3rd Ukrainian Front that had been fighting strong German attacks around Budapest since the beginning of the month. The Western Carpathian offensive ended on February 18, having destroyed 17 Hungarian and German divisions and knocked out about 320 German and Hungarian tanks and assault guns. Soviet losses included about 360 tanks and assault guns and some 590,000 Soviet and Romanian casualties.

The third of the January offensives was the East Prussian operation, conducted primarily by the 2nd and 3rd Belorussian Fronts. This involved seven tank corps, one mechanized corps, and ten independent tank brigades, with a total of 3,859 tanks and assault guns. Facing them were elements of Heeresgruppen Mitte and Nord, with about 700 Panzers and AFVs. Although the offensive managed to isolate the Prussian capital of Königsberg, the city remained in German hands until April 9 after enduring a prolonged and costly siege. Soviet casualties on this front through the end of April 1945 totaled 1.7 million killed and wounded, along with 3,525 tanks and assault guns.

An IS-2m heavy tank of Lieutenant Colonel M. A. Oglobin's 34th Guards Heavy Tank Regiment during the fighting for Festung Posen in January 1945. Tanks of this unit were responsible for knocking out the Panther located on Horst Wesel Platz shown in the photo above. Note that this tank has lost one of its road wheels on the right side.

**ABOVE LEFT**
A column of SU-85M assault guns of the 2nd Belorussian Front in January 1945 during the East Prussia offensive. This is the later type of SU-85 with the revised superstructure that included a cupola for the vehicle commander.

**ABOVE RIGHT**
A Jagdpanzer 38(t) of the Heeres-Panzerjäger-Abteilung.731 in Kurland in February 1945. This was the first unit equipped with these vehicles on the Russian Front in the summer of 1944. Unofficially called the "Hetzer" in some units, these generally were deployed in the Panzerjäger-Abteilungen of infantry divisions, but were sometimes deployed with corps-level tank destroyer units.

Heeresgruppe Kurland on the Baltic coast in Latvia remained isolated from the rest of the Wehrmacht at the start of the Soviet January offensives. This formation included the 4.Panzer-Division. Hitler refused to evacuate the troops there, arguing that they tied down Red Army forces. However, the Red Army kept the pocket isolated using second-rate formations and started some half-hearted efforts in February 1945 to whittle down the German bridgehead. The pocket did not surrender until May 1945.

While the 3rd Belorussian Front was tied down around Königsberg, the 2nd Belorussian Front, as well as elements of the 1st Belorussian Front, were instructed to clear out the Pomeranian corridor up to the Baltic Sea. Starting on February 10, this operation involved seven tank corps, three mechanized corps, three independent tank brigades, and one independent assault gun brigade. The port of Danzig finally fell on March 30, 1945. The 2nd Belorussian Front that bore the brunt of the fighting suffered about 560,000 casualties, as well as the loss of 680 tanks and assault guns. About 20 German divisions, mainly from Heeresgruppe Weichsel, were destroyed.

## *Spring Awakening* in Hungary

Hitler, incensed by the fall of Budapest, ordered the city to be retaken. Operation *Frühlingserwachen* (*Spring Awakening*) was launched by Heeresgruppe Süd on March 6, 1945. The main strike force was Dietrich's 6.SS-Panzer-Armee, modestly re-equipped since the Ardennes debacle in December 1944. For this offensive, the corps' four Panzer

**A**

### 1. TIGER I, 10./PANZER-REGIMENT GD, PANZERGRENADIER-DIVISION GROSSDEUTSCHLAND, EAST PRUSSIA, JANUARY 1945

This Tiger I served in the III. (*schwere*) Abteilung of the Panzer-Regiment Grossdeutschland. The three Tiger companies of this battalion used their own tactical numbering systems, with 9.Kompanie starting with the letter "A," 10.Kompanie with "B," and 11.Kompanie with "C," followed by the two-digit tank number. The camouflage pattern on this tank has been hastily broken up with whitewash. The standard vehicle camouflage adopted in 1943 consisted of a base finish of RAL 7028 dark yellow, with patches of RAL 6003 olive green and RAL 8017 red brown applied by the unit in the field or depots issuing the tanks.

### 2. TIGER I OF 3./S.PZ.ABT.507, PRASCHNITZ (PRZASNYSZ), JANUARY 1945

The s.Pz.Abt.507 had a unique style of tactical numbers, with the company number being considerably larger than the two following tank numbers. The battalion had fastened extra track links to the sides of the turret since 1944, and the tactical numbers overlapped the spare track. The camouflage pattern on this tank is extremely indistinct.

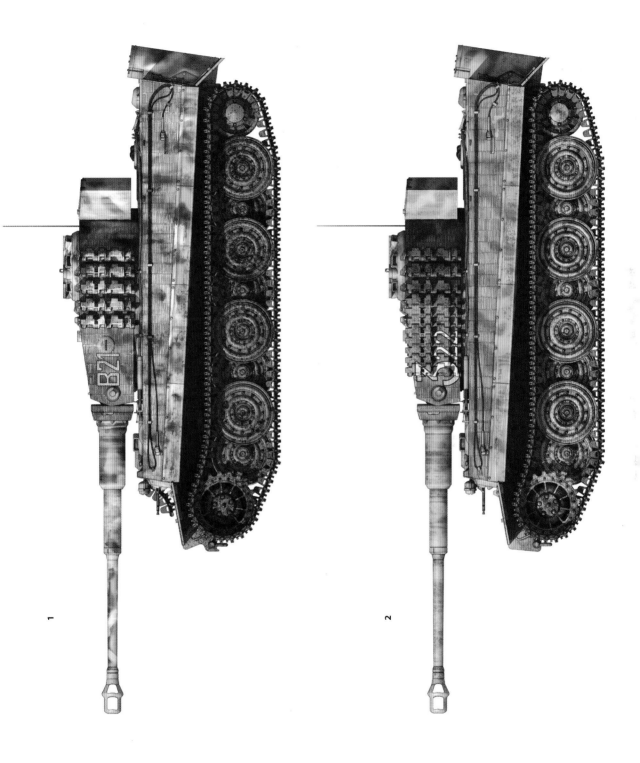

1

2

divisions had a total of 278 tanks and AFVs, including 87 PzKpfw IVs, 61 Panthers, nine King Tigers (Tiger IIs), and 80 Pz IV/L70s. This was only about half the strength the corps had at the start of the Ardennes offensive.

| **Operational Panzer strength, Heeresgrupe Süd, March 5, 1945\*** | | | | | |
|---|---|---|---|---|---|
| **Pz IV** | **Panther** | **Tiger** | **PzJg** | **StuG** | **Total** |
| 135 | 249 | 104 | 94 | 176 | 758 |

\*A further 167 tanks and 99 StuG/Panzerjäger assault and self-propelled guns in repair

Facing this offensive was the 3rd Ukrainian Front. Although Red Army intelligence was aware of German preparations for an offensive in the Budapest sector, resources were being shifted to other operations and the local Soviet commanders were warned that they would have to make do with available resources. Soviet defenses relied on antitank artillery. This was one theater where the Germans had a decided advantage in armor strength.

| **Tanks and AFVs of the 3rd Ukrainian Front, March 5, 1945** | | | | | | | | |
|---|---|---|---|---|---|---|---|---|
| | **T-34** | **M4A2** | **IS-2** | **SU-76** | **SU-100** | **ISU-122** | **ISU-152** | **Total** |
| Operational | 157 | 47 | 4 | 95 | 78 | 23 | 9 | 413 |
| In repair | 4 | 1 | 0 | 0 | 2 | 1 | 1 | 9 |
| **Total** | **161** | **48** | **4** | **95** | **80** | **24** | **10** | **422** |

The *Spring Awakening* offensive penetrated nearly 18 miles (30km) into Soviet lines, but was eventually halted by the Soviet antitank defenses. The Wehrmacht's offensive momentum was largely exhausted in a week of fighting. The 3rd Ukrainian Front claimed 533 tanks, StuGs and Panzerjägers at the end of the offensive, about half of the attacking force. This was the last major German Panzer offensive of the war.

A camouflaged Panther Ausf G tank of 1. SS-Panzer-Division "Leibstandarte Adolf Hitler" during the fighting against the Soviet bridgehead over the Gran River in Hungary on February 26, 1945.

A pair of whitewashed SU-76Ms of the 4th Ukrainian Front in action in the Carpathian Mountains along the Slovak–Hungarian border in February 1945.

**German tanks and AFVs claimed by 3rd Ukrainian Front, March 6–15, 1945**

|  | Destroyed | Disabled, abandoned | Total |
|---|---|---|---|
| 4th Guards Army |  | 7 | 7 |
| 26th Army | 186 | 13 | 199 |
| 27th Army | 104 | 162 | 266 |
| 57th Army | 34 | 27 | 61 |
| **Total** | **324** | **209** | **533** |

**Strength of Panzer units on Russian Front, March 15, 1945**

|  | Operational | In repair | Total |
|---|---|---|---|
| Pzkpw IV | 345 | 248 | 593 |
| Pz IV/70 | 189 | 168 | 357 |
| Panther | 387 | 389 | 776 |
| Tiger | 125 | 87 | 212 |
| StuG | 314 | 231 | 545 |
| Flak Pz | 50 | 47 | 97 |
| **Total** | **1,410** | **1,170** | **2,580** |

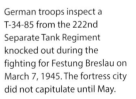

German troops inspect a T-34-85 from the 222nd Separate Tank Regiment knocked out during the fighting for Festung Breslau on March 7, 1945. The fortress city did not capitulate until May.

The defeat of the *Spring Awakening* offensive led the Red Army to respond with its own operation towards Vienna on March 16, involving the 3rd Ukrainian Front and elements of the 2nd Ukrainian Front. The armored components included three tank corps, three mechanized corps, one independent mechanized brigade, and one independent assault gun brigade. The spearheads of both fronts were special assault groups, with the 3rd Ukrainian Front group having 197 tanks and assault guns and the 2nd Ukrainian Front group another 165. After an intense urban battle,

Vienna fell to the Red Army late on April 10. Soviet losses amounted to 920,500 killed and wounded as well as 603 tanks and assault guns. The Red Army claimed 1,300 Panzers and AFVs captured or destroyed, along with 130,000 prisoners of war. Hitler was so angered by the performance of the Waffen-SS Panzer divisions of the 6.SS-Panzer-Armee in this operation that he instructed their troops to remove their honorific cuff bands.

An elephant's graveyard of derelict German Panzers in the Vienna Arsenal in April 1945 after the capture of the city by the Red Army. In the foreground is the usual assortment of Panther and Tiger tanks, but farther back are a number of war-booty tanks (*Beutepanzer*), including a French Renault FT and a few Italian M14/41s. The war-booty tanks were typically used by anti-partisan security units.

### The battle for Berlin

The final battle for Berlin began on April 16. The German defenses consisted of five lines, starting at the Seelow Heights to the east of the capital. The principal German forces on the Berlin axis were Heeresgruppen Weichsel and Mitte. These two army groups, plus the Berlin garrison, comprised 770,000 German troops, along with 425 tanks and 1,070 assault guns and tank destroyers for a total of 1,495 AFVs. One of the more curious tank formations was Panzerkompanie (*bodenständige*) Berlin, an improvised unit formed in February 1945 and equipped with ten derelict Panther and 12 PzKpfw IV tanks with functional weapons that were buried as static defenses at key road junctions within Berlin.

| Operational Panzer strength, April 10, 1945* | | | | | | |
|---|---|---|---|---|---|---|
| Heeresgruppe | Kurland | Weichsel | Mitte | Süd | Südost | Total |
| Pz III | 2 | 2 | 3 | 7 | | 14 |
| Pz IV | 3 | 102 | 71 | 51 | | 227 |
| Pz IV (lg) | 14 | 10 | 113 | 35 | | 172 |
| Panther | 30 | 83 | 116 | 45 | | 274 |
| Tiger | 13 | 46 | 1 | 21 | | 81 |
| StuG III | 129 | 202 | 215 | 69 | 19 | 634 |
| StuG IV | 61 | 20 | 29 | 18 | | 128 |
| StuH | 21 | 38 | 15 | 14 | 3 | 91 |
| Jagd.Pz 38(t) | 13 | 187 | 198 | 84 | 9 | 491 |
| Nashorn | | | 39 | | | 39 |
| Jagdpanther | | | 5 | 6 | | 11 |
| Art.Bef.Wg. | | | 8 | 11 | | 19 |
| Flak Pz | | 17 | 15 | 19 | | 51 |
| Berge Pz | 10 | | | 20 | | 30 |
| Beute Pz | 1 | 20 | 11 | | 27 | 59 |
| Beute StuG | 2 | | | | 26 | 28 |
| Total | 299 | 727 | 839 | 400 | 84 | 2,349 |

*Heeresgruppe Nord not included due to lack of report

The Red Army's Berlin operation was conducted primarily by the 1st and 2nd Belorussian Fronts and 1st Ukrainian Front. These eventually included 13 tank corps, seven mechanized corps, nine independent tank brigades, and six independent assault gun brigades, with a total of about 6,250 tanks and assault guns.

A Panther Ausf G, probably from Pz.Rgt.29 of Panzer-Division Müncheberg, knocked out along the Kietz–Golzow road on March 27 or 28, 1945, during the second and final attempt to relieve the besieged Festung Küstrin garrison.

The assault began with Zhukov's 1st Belorussian Front attacking the heavily fortified Seelow Heights. Some idea of the ferocity of the fighting can be appreciated from the scale of Soviet tank losses during this initial breakthrough operation.

| 1st Belorussian Front tank and AFV casualties at the Seelow Heights | | | | |
|---|---|---|---|---|
|  | Destroyed | Knocked out | Other | Total |
| April 14 | 31 | 29 | 29 | 89 |
| April 15 | 15 | 10 | 9 | 34 |
| April 16 | 71 | 77 | 40 | 188 |
| April 17 | 79 | 85 | 15 | 179 |
| April 18 | 65 | 86 | 13 | 164 |
| April 19 | 105 | 76 | 8 | 189 |
| April 20 | 83 | 81 | 5 | 169 |
| **Total** | **449** | **444** | **119** | **1,012** |

An ISU-122 of the 375th Guards Heavy Self-propelled Artillery Regiment, 3rd Guards Tank Corps, moving through the streets of Danzig (Gdansk) in early April 1945, days after the capture of the port city by the 2nd Belorussian Front on March 30, 1945.

By Hitler's birthday, April 20, the Soviet spearheads had reached the outer approaches of Berlin. On April 25, Zhukov's 1st Belorussian Front and Konev's 1st Ukrainian Front completed the encirclement of the city, meeting in the southwest suburbs of Berlin. By the following day, the Red Army was heavily engaged in street fighting inside Berlin. The Soviet tactics stressed firepower over manpower. There were ample numbers of tanks and assault guns to provide direct fire support, and both divisional and corps artillery guns were dragged

into Berlin and used in a direct-fire mode to reduce buildings. Even though the German defenders were grossly outnumbered, urban combat was a time-consuming and costly business.

Some sense of the dynamics of Soviet tank casualties can be gathered from the accompanying chart showing AFV strength of the 11th Guards Tank Corps, 1st Guards Tank Army, during the Seelow Heights–Berlin fighting. As can be seen, units like these took significant losses during the initial breakthrough operation on the Seelow Heights so that by the time they reached Berlin around April 26, they were down to only about 40 percent of their initial strength. Of these casualties, 116 were total losses and the rest were repairable.

| 11th Guards Tank Corps' tank and AFV strength, April 16 to May 2, 1945 | | | | | | | | |
|---|---|---|---|---|---|---|---|---|
| | T-34 | IS-2 | SU-100 | SU-85 | SU-76 | SU-57 | ISU-122 | Total |
| **April** | | | | | | | | |
| **16** | 135 | 1 | 13 | 8 | 16 | 3 | 20 | 196 |
| **17** | 138 | 1 | 13 | 8 | 17 | 3 | 20 | 200 |
| **18** | 117 | 1 | 11 | 7 | 17 | 2 | 20 | 175 |
| **19** | 97 | | 10 | 5 | 17 | 2 | 20 | 151 |
| **20** | 76 | | 9 | 6 | 10 | 2 | 19 | 122 |
| **21** | 62 | | 9 | 5 | 9 | 2 | 19 | 106 |
| **22** | 58 | | 10 | 6 | 10 | 2 | 19 | 105 |
| **23** | 57 | | 8 | 5 | 10 | 2 | 18 | 100 |
| **24** | 52 | | 9 | 5 | 9 | 2 | 16 | 93 |
| **25** | 51 | | 9 | 5 | 9 | 2 | | 76 |
| **26** | 48 | | 10 | 7 | 9 | 2 | | 76 |
| **27** | 43 | | 8 | 5 | 8 | 2 | | 66 |
| **28** | 45 | | 8 | 5 | 8 | 2 | | 68 |
| **29** | 42 | | 10 | 5 | 8 | 2 | | 67 |
| **30** | 34 | | 10 | 6 | 8 | 5 | | 63 |
| **May** | | | | | | | | |
| **1** | 36 | | 10 | 3 | 7 | | | 56 |
| **2** | 44 | | 9 | 4 | 7 | 2 | | 66 |

**B**

**1. ISU-122, 375TH GUARDS HEAVY SELF-PROPELLED ARTILLERY REGIMENT, 3RD GUARDS TANK CORPS, DANZIG, APRIL 1945**

Soviet vehicles in World War II were painted in 4BO camouflage green, a very dark and dull green color. The Red Army made increasing use of tactical insignia in the final year of the war, mainly as a method of traffic control. The patterns were usually unique to each tank army or tank corps, and were random to frustrate German intelligence. The 3rd Guards Tank Corps used a geometric symbol of a circle within a tombstone-shaped outline. Below this was a two-digit number indicating the subunit within the corps, in this case "17" for the 375th Guards Heavy SP Artillery Regiment. This is accompanied by a three-digit tactical number indicating the battalion and vehicle number.

**2. ISU-152, 262ND GUARDS HEAVY SELF-PROPELLED ARTILLERY REGIMENT, 25TH TANK CORPS, COTTBUS, GERMANY, APRIL 1945**

This ISU-152 assault gun carries two slogans: "Vpered na Berlin!" (*Forward to Berlin*) on the gun barrel and "Daësh Berlin" (*Give Up Berlin*) on the superstructure side. The unit tactical marking is also carried on the hull side, along with the vehicle tactical number. The tactical markings of the 25th Tank Corps are not well documented, but appear to have used a variety of circular insignia with two horizontal stripes below.

1

2

A column of StuG III Ausf Gs of StuG-Brigade.301 that surrendered in Slovakia in April 1945 to the 4th Ukrainian Front. These vehicles have had thin steel plates added to the side of the sponsons over the mudguards, although it is not clear if this was intended as spaced armor or for additional stowage.

**BELOW LEFT**
A pair of SU-76M assault guns of the 3rd Belorussian Front advance through the streets of Königsberg in April 1945 during the final street fighting for the Prussian capital.

**BELOW RIGHT**
The T-34-85 commanded by Lieutenant L. E. Burakov of the 1st Battalion, 63rd Guards Tank Brigade, 10th Guards Tank Corps, in the Klárov district of Prague below Prague castle. This unit was ambushed by several Jagdpanzer 38(t) tank destroyers serving as a rearguard for retreating German units, knocking out Lieutenant Goncharenko's T-34-85, number 1-23. The Soviet tanks in turn knocked out at least one of the Jagdpanzer 38(t)s, seen in the photo on page 22.

Unwilling to surrender, Hitler appointed Admiral Karl Dönitz as his successor and committed suicide in his bunker on the afternoon of April 30. On May 1, the German Army chief of staff made contact with Soviet forces in Berlin to begin negotiating for the surrender. The ceasefire did not come into effect in Berlin until the afternoon of May 2, fighting continuing in isolated pockets around the city for several days. Soviet casualties in the Berlin operation were about 81,000 killed and 280,000 wounded. Red Army losses also included nearly 2,000 tanks and assault guns, almost a third of the armored force. The Red Army estimated that German casualties were 538,000 killed and 520,000 wounded.

Although the siege of Berlin sealed the fate of Nazi Germany, it was not the last major operation of the war. The Wehrmacht still had a substantial force in the Czech provinces and controlled the capital,

Prague. Czech resistance forces staged an uprising in Prague on May 5 and called for help. On the night of May 8/9, Konev ordered the 3rd and 4th Tank Armies to make a dash for Prague. In spite of the surrender of the German government on the night of May 8/9, fighting continued in the Czech lands for several more days. The 2nd and 4th Ukrainian Fronts reinforced Konev's forces in the fighting near Prague on May 9 and 10. Some isolated German garrisons such as the Kurland pocket did not surrender until the second week of May.

# DOCTRINE AND ORGANIZATION

### Wehrmacht

German tank and AFV losses in 1944 on all fronts totaled 11,979, according to studies by GenMaj Hermann Burkhart Müller-Hillebrand. This figure appears to be significantly low, since OKH records suggest that losses on the Russian Front alone were nearly that high. In the event, by the end of 1944, Soviet tank strength was more than four times higher than overall German tank strength and 14 times higher than deployed German strength on the Eastern Front. A significant reason for this disparity was Hitler's decision to commit much of the Wehrmacht's Panzer reserves to the Western Front in December 1944 for his ill-fated Ardennes offensive.

| German tank and AFV inventory, January 1, 1945 | |
| --- | --- |
| Overall tank inventory | 6,284 |
| Deployable tank inventory | 5,670 |
| Overall StuG inventory | 6,155 |
| Deployable StuG inventory | 5,930 |
| Deployable Panzerjäger inventory | 736 |
| **Total inventory** | **13,175** |
| **Total deployable** | **12,336** |

This Panther Befehlswagen was one of 22 static tank pillboxes of Panzerkompanie (bodenständige) Berlin. It was emplaced in the Charlottenburg district of Berlin at the junction of Bismarckstrasse, looking towards Kaiserdamm. It has suffered numerous penetrations of its armor during the Berlin street fighting.

The defeat of the Ardennes offensive between December 1944 and January 1945 marked a reversal in German tank deployment patterns. Although the Western Front had been favored in overall tank deployment as well as the supply of tanks from May–December 1944, this was reversed in January 1945 to face the renewed Soviet offensive along the Berlin axis. The 6.SS-Panzer-Armee was transferred from the Ardennes to the Russian Front to take part in German counterattacks in the Lake Balaton and Budapest sectors in Hungary. As a result of this transfer, nearly all of the Waffen-SS, except for the 17.SS-Panzergrenadier-Division, was committed to the Eastern Front.

The accompanying chart shows the overall total German Panzer and AFV strength, comparing East versus West. The discrepancy between this chart and the previous chart on overall strength is due to the deployment of Panzers on secondary fronts as well as Panzers retained in Germany for training and unit reconstruction.

| Panzer strength: East vs West, January 15, 1945 | | | |
|---|---|---|---|
| | **West** | **East** | **Total** |
| Operational Panzers | 979 | 1,175 | 2,154 |
| Panzers in repair | 646 | 589 | 1,235 |
| Panzers in delivery | 342 | 486 | 828 |
| *Panzer subtotal* | *1,967* | *2,250* | *4,217* |
| Operational StuGs | 605 | 1,820 | 2,425 |
| StuGs in repair | 455 | 402 | 857 |
| StuGs in delivery | 280 | 434 | 714 |
| *StuG subtotal* | *1,340* | *2,656* | *3,996* |
| **Total** | **3,307** | **4,906** | **8,213** |

The Panzer balance continued to shift in favor of the Russian Front through the rest of 1945, while strength in the West continued to decline. For example, in November and December 1944, a total of 2,197 new Panzers and AFVs were delivered to the West, compared to only 919 in the East; but from January–March 1945, the trend reversed with the West receiving only 544 Panzers and AFVs compared to 3,086 in the East.

**Distribution of new Panzers and AFVs, 1945**

| East | Jan | Feb | Mar | Total |
|---|---|---|---|---|
| Pz IV | 120 | 194 | 55 | 369 |
| Pz IV Lg (A) | 37 | 49 | 16 | 102 |
| Panther | 154 | 178 | 50 | 382 |
| Tiger | 55 | 45 | 13 | 113 |
| StuG | 431 | 382 | 122 | 935 |
| Pz IV Lg (V) | 98 | 227 | 28 | 353 |
| Jagdpanther | 42 | 48 | | 90 |
| Jagdpanzer 38(t) | 327 | 332 | 83 | 742 |
| **Total** | **1,264** | **1,455** | **367** | **3,086** |

The Wehrmacht on the Russian Front was organized in the traditional fashion. The basic operational formation was the Heeresgruppe (*army group*) consisting of several corps. Although there were several Panzer-Korps in the order of battle, these did not have the high density of Panzer divisions seen during the campaigns of 1939–41.

In mid-January 1945, the bulk of Germany's Panzer and Panzergrenadier divisions were deployed on the Russian Front. This included 20 of the 33 Panzer divisions and nine of the 14 Panzergrenadier divisions. The deployment pattern is detailed in the accompanying chart. As will be noted, Heeresgruppe Süd, located primarily in Hungary, had nearly half of the Panzer strength in the east due to the prolonged battles around Budapest that had started in the autumn of 1944 and continued through to the spring of 1945.

**Panzer divisions on the Russian Front, January 21, 1945**

| | Panzer divisions | Panzergrenadier divisions | Total |
|---|---|---|---|
| HG Nord | 3 | 1.5 | 4.5 |
| HG Mitte | 2 | 3 | 5 |
| HG A | 5 | 3 | 8 |
| HG Süd | 10 | 1.5 | 11.5 |
| **Total** | **20** | **9** | **29** |

A Tiger I of 3./s.Pz.Abt.507 near Przasnysz, Poland, being inspected by Soviet troops in late January 1945. This tank broke down in the middle of that month during the fighting along the southern border between Poland and East Prussia, and was scuttled by its crew on January 16 after it could not be recovered. The battalion lost most of its Tigers by early February and was sent back to Paderborn for refitting with new Tiger II tanks. This battalion used a distinctive style of tactical numbers on the turret, with the initial Kompanie number larger than the subsequent numerals.

The Panzer divisions were generally organized on the 1944 *Kriegsstärkenachweisungen* (war establishment strength). However, few Panzer divisions actually matched the objectives of the organizational charts that authorized about 165 tanks per division. In late 1944, the General Inspector of the Panzer Force issued lower temporary guidelines for the Panzer strength of various divisions, hoping to create at least a minimum strength for the divisions. In mid-January 1945, there were only about 1,765 Panzers deployed on the Russian Front, compared to a paper requirement for around 3,330. In early January 1945, the average Panzer division had about 55 Panzers, or roughly a third of its authorized strength. On January 5, 1945, Panzer divisions on the Russian Front had an immediate shortfall of 534 Panzers and 134 Sturmgeschütze, not counting the three Panther and one PzKpfw IV battalions that had not yet arrived.

| Divisional Panzer strength, January 5, 1945 | | | | |
|---|---|---|---|---|
| | Pz IV | Panther | StuG | Total |
| **HG Nord** | | | | |
| 4.Pz.Div. | 41 | 48 | 13 | 102 |
| 12.Pz.Div. | 25 | | 47 | 72 |
| 14.Pz.Div. | 13 | 44 | 16 | 73 |
| **HG Mitte** | | | | |
| 5.Pz.Div. | 31 | 43 | 41 | 115 |
| 7.Pz.Div. | 46 | 39 | | 85 |
| 24.Pz.Div. | | | 21 | 21 |
| Pz.Div.HG | 38 | 45 | 17 | 100 |
| Pz.Gr.Div.HG | | | 32 | 32 |
| 18.Pz.Gr.Div. | | | 45 | 45 |
| Pz.Div.GD* | | 24 | 41 | 65 |
| Pz.Gr.Div.Brandenburg | | | 21 | 21 |
| **HG A** | | | | |
| 16.Pz.Div. | 23 | 58 | 17 | 98 |
| 17.Pz.Div. | 80 | | 21 | 101 |
| 19.Pz.Div. | 53 | 33 | 21 | 107 |
| 25.Pz.Div. | 38 | 28 | 21 | 87 |
| 10.Pz.Gren.Div. | | | 37 | 37 |
| 20.Pz.Gr.Div. | | | 49 | 49 |
| **HG Süd** | | | | |
| 1.Pz.Div. | 14 | 38 | 2 | 54 |
| 3.Pz.Div. | 32 | 47 | 23 | 102 |
| 6.Pz.Div. | 24 | 46 | 12 | 82 |
| 8.Pz.Div. | 18 | 42 | 12 | 72 |
| 13.Pz.Div. | 7 | 7 | 21 | 35 |
| 20.Pz.Div. | 52 | 35 | 19 | 106 |
| 23.Pz.Div. | 16 | 26 | 24 | 66 |
| SS-Pz.Div.Totenkopf* | 31 | 29 | 50 | 110 |
| SS-Pz.Div.Viking | 14 | 29 | 18 | 61 |
| Pz.Div.FH | | 9 | 13 | 22 |
| **Total** | **596** | **670** | **654** | **1,920** |

*Grossdeutschland also had 15 Tigers; Totenkopf had 11 Tigers on strength.

Besides these divisions, in mid-January, the 6.SS-Panzer-Armee was transferred from the Ardennes to Heeresgruppe Süd in Hungary. The accompanying chart shows the unit strength shortly before its transfer. The divisional totals include attached units such as s.SS-Pz.Abt.501 with 1.SS-Pz. Div. and Pz.Jag.Abt.560 with the 12.SS-Pz.Div. The 10.SS-Pz.Div. that had been deployed in Alsace for the Operation *Nordwind* offensive is included in this chart since it was also transferred to the East.

| 6.SS-Panzer-Armee Panzer strength, January 8, 1945 | | | | | | | |
|---|---|---|---|---|---|---|---|
| | Pz IV | Panther | Tiger | Pz IV L | StuG | Jagdpanther | Total |
| 1.SS-Pz.Div. | 24 | 36 | 26 | 11 | | | 97 |
| 2.SS-Pz.Div. | 14 | 34 | | 10 | 12 | | 70 |
| 9.SS-Pz.Div. | 21 | 30 | | 9 | 17 | | 77 |
| 10.SS-Pz.Div. | 36 | 38 | | 20 | | | 94 |
| 12.SS-Pz.Div. | 20 | 26 | | 29 | | 6 | 81 |
| **Total** | **115** | **164** | **26** | **79** | **29** | **6** | **419** |

Since it was unlikely that enough new tanks would be provided to raise the Panzer divisions to the 1944 KStN war establishment levels, the General Inspector of Panzer Troops proposed two new divisional structures. "Panzer Division 1945" consolidated the two tank battalions of the 1944 Panzer regiment into a single battalion, and the authorized tank strength fell from 165 to just 54 tanks. Instead of remaining as a homogenous tank unit, the 1945 Panzer Regiment would also include a Panzergrenadier Bataillon (*gepanzerte*) with the infantry riding armored halftracks. The division's two Panzergrenadier regiments were to be converted into motorized infantry regiments without halftracks. As a result, the 1945 division was authorized only 90 armored halftracks compared to 288 in the 1944 division.

In the face of heavy losses during the early 1945 campaigns, on April 1, the General Inspector of the Panzer Troops authorized yet another KStN. This was intended to reorganize Panzer divisions that were too weak to meet even the destitute Panzer Division 1945 authorizations. The new "Kampfgruppe/ Panzer Division 1945" had an authorized strength of 8,602 men, 54 tanks, 22 Jagdpanzer tank destroyers, and 90 armored halftracks. However, these new organizational structures could not be followed due to the chaos of the final months of the war. As a result, Panzer and Panzergrenadier divisions used the usual practice of combining the remnants of available combat formations into improvised *Kampfgruppen* (battle groups).

The Panzergrenadier divisions were organized in a similar fashion to the Panzer divisions, but they had a smaller Panzer component, with only one Panzer battalion versus the Panzer regiment with two battalions in the Panzer division. By 1945, each division's Panzer battalion was usually equipped with StuGs rather than Panzers. As in the case of the Panzer divisions, the Panzergrenadier divisions suffered from perennial shortages of equipment.

The best-known Panzer units aside from the Panzer divisions were the Tiger heavy tank battalions (s.Pz.Abt.: *schwere Panzerabteilung*). These were subordinate to the Heeresgruppe, though in practice they were usually assigned to corps during the campaigns. A total of 11 Heer and three Waffen-SS battalions were formed during the war, of which nearly all surviving battalions served on the Russian Front in 1945, except for s.Pz. Abt.506 in western Germany and s.Pz.Abt.508 in Italy. Due to their combat effectiveness, these battalions were in constant demand. Not surprisingly,

This Jagdpanzer 38(t) was involved in one of the most famous tank duels of the Prague uprising, knocking out the first Soviet tank to reach Prague, Lieutenant Goncharenko's T-34-85. It was quickly knocked out by other tanks of Goncharenko's unit. In the background is the famous Pražský hrad, Prague's royal castle.

they suffered considerable losses in the process. The decline in strength was accelerated by mechanical problems, especially with the heavier Tiger II. The Allied bombing of the main Tiger plant at Kassel in 1944 meant that there was a continual shortage of replacement Tigers and spare parts. Endemic reliability problems with the Tigers often resulted in more Tigers being lost due to breakdown and abandonment than to enemy action. The usual Wehrmacht practice was to allow the battalions to shrink to only a few vehicles due to combat attrition, then withdraw the battalion back into Germany for re-equipment. This process led to the gradual extinction of the Tiger I and its replacement by the new Tiger II in the spring of 1945.

The most numerous armored vehicles on the Russian Front were the various types of assault guns. These were divided between separate assault gun units such as the Sturmgeschütz-Brigaden and divisional units such as the Panzerjäger-Abteilungen in the infantry divisions. Although called brigades, the Sturmgeschütz units were in fact closer to battalions in size, averaging less than 30 assault guns each at the start of the 1945 campaign. It is worth noting that besides the usual StuG III and StuG IV, some of these units received the Pz IV/70(A) instead. The Panzerjäger-Abteilung in select infantry divisions had a company of assault guns, usually the Jagdpanzer 38(t).

| Sturmgeschütz brigades on the Russian Front, January 5, 1945 | | |
|---|---|---|
| | Number of brigades | Number of StuGs |
| Heeresgruppe Nord | 6 | 182 |
| Heeresgruppe Mitte | 13 | 391 |
| Heeresgruppe A | 7 | ? |
| Heeresgruppe Süd | 5 | 102 |
| **Total** | **31** | **>675** |

**C**

### 1. BEFEHLSPANTHER AUSF G, STAB KOMPANIE, FALLSCHIRM-PANZER-REGIMENT.1 "HERMANN GORING," EAST PRUSSIA, 1945

This was the command tank of Major Karl Rossmann, decorated with the Knights Cross with Oak Leaves in February 1945. It has the typical command tactical number "R01" in black with white trim. The regimental centaur insignia was painted in white on the lower right corner of the glacis plate. This command tank was manufactured at Maschinenfabrik Augsburg-Nürnberg GmbH (MAN) in September/October 1944 and had the chassis number 121081 painted centrally on the glacis plate. In the late summer of 1944, the Wehrmacht changed its vehicle camouflage practices, substituting factory-applied camouflage patterns instead of the previous system of allowing units to apply their own camouflage. These camouflage schemes often followed certain patterns from factory to factory. The camouflage pattern here was typical for MAN during the autumn of 1944, except that the side skirts are in a different "ambush" pattern. The gun barrel appears to have been replaced by a new one that was left in the dark grey heat-resistant primer.

### 2. PANTHER AUSF G, 1./SS-PANZER-REGIMENT.1, 1.SS-PANZER-DIVISION LSSAH, HUNGARY, MARCH 1945

This Panther Ausf G was abandoned near the Székesfehrvár railway station between Lake Balaton and Budapest at the end of the fighting in Hungary in March 1945. It was finished in the camouflage pattern typical of Panthers manufactured by Maschinenfabrik Niedersachsen GmbH (MNH) in the late autumn of 1944. The barrel was replaced and left in the original heat-resistant grey primer. The small black tactical numbers are typical of the 1.SS-Panzer-Division in 1944 and 1945.

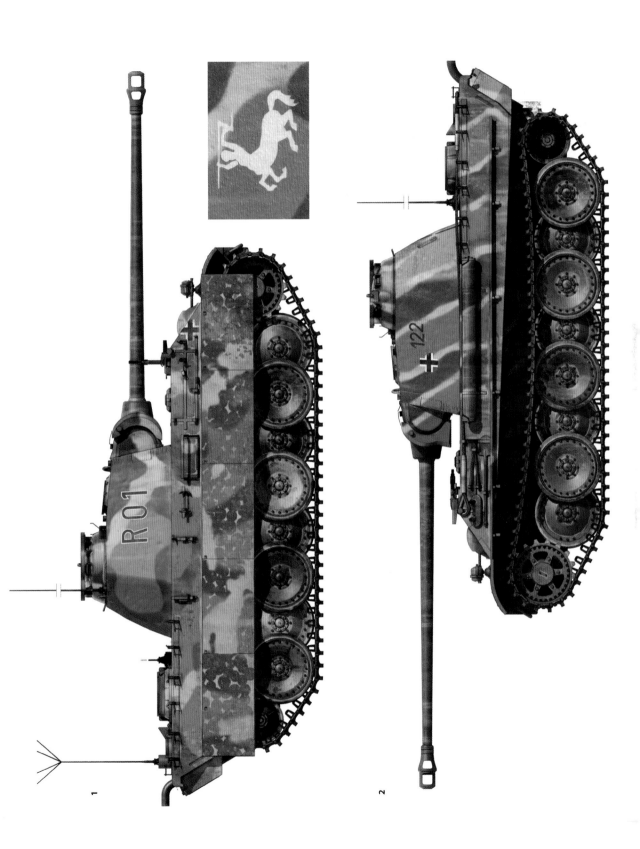

1

2

A column of abandoned StuG IV assault guns along with a 105mm LFh 18/40 field gun in the Elbing sector of the 2nd Belorussian Front in East Prussia in January 1945 during the fighting along the Baltic coast.

There were a number of different types of tank destroyer units in service in 1945. The heavy tank destroyer battalions (*schwere-Panzerjäger-Abteilungen*) were equipped with the 88mm Nashorn or Jagdpanther. A larger formation, the Panzerjäger-Brigade, was first formed in January 1945 with the intention of creating a concentrated formation to counterattack Soviet tank breakthroughs. On paper, these brigades consisted of six battalions. The first of these, Panzerjäger-Brigade.104, was formed in Berlin in late January 1945. In practice, it was broken up and its component battalions were deployed separately. Several other tank destroyer brigades were formed in March and April 1945, but their combat record remains obscure.

## German allies

Germany's last major remaining ally in the East was Hungary. During the course of the war, the Hungarian Army fielded two armored divisions.[1] Some other units, such as the 1st Cavalry (later Hussar) Division, had an armored component. There were also a number of small formations for infantry support, including assault gun battalions. These were equipped primarily with Hungarian AFVs, the Toldi light tank, based on a Swedish Landsverk design, and the Turán, based on a Czechoslovak medium tank design. Arguably the best Hungarian vehicle was the Zrinyi assault gun, based on the Turán medium tank and mounting a 105mm howitzer. Hungary was developing its own Panther equivalent, the Tas, but the sole prototype was destroyed by an American bombing raid on the factory in 1944, putting an end to the program.

Berlin was never enthusiastic about supplying its own tanks to its allies, and grudgingly sold Hungary some PzKpfw 38(t)s and PzKpfw IVs. Given the obsolescence of most Hungarian tanks, Germany transferred a small

1    Steven Zaloga, *Tanks of Hitler's Eastern Allies 1941–45*, Osprey New Vanguard 199 (2013).

During February 1945, some elements of the Hungarian 3rd Tank Regiment, 2nd Armored Division, withdrew into neighboring Slovakia near Bratislava. They destroyed much of the remaining equipment, such as this 40M Turán medium tank that is missing its gun. This tank has been fitted with the Hungarian version of side skirts which, unlike the German Schurzen, was made of sheet steel with a pattern of small drilled holes. This tank was subsequently captured by units of the 4th Ukrainian Front.

number of more modern AFVs to Hungary in the final year of the war, including StuG IIIs, Jagdpanzer 38(t)s, and a few Tigers and Panthers. The Hungarian 1st Armored Division and 1st Hussar Division took part in the battles on the approaches to Budapest starting in late October 1944, while the 2nd Armored Division and Billnizter Group fought south of the city in the engagements near Lake Balaton. Much of the Hungarian armored force was encircled and destroyed in the four months of fighting around Budapest, which finally fell to the Red Army on February 13, 1945. The 1st Hussar Division escaped the encirclement west of Budapest and finally surrendered in late March. Some elements of the 2nd Armored Division fought to the northwest of the city along the Danube, and small parts of the division withdrew towards Bratislava in neighboring Slovakia, where they were destroyed by their crews. One of the last major Hungarian armored actions of the war involved the Jagdpanzer 38(t) of the 20th and 25th Assault Gun Battalions, which took part in the Wehrmacht's desperate *Frühlingserwachen* counteroffensive in the Lake Balaton region in early March 1945.

One of the most obscure of Germany's eastern allies was General A. A. Vlasov's Russian Liberation Army (ROA: *Russkaya Osvoboditelnaya Armiya*), formed from Soviet prisoners of war. This formation had a small armored component equipped with 1941-era Soviet equipment, including a few T-34 tanks and BA-10 armored cars. Hitler and other senior Wehrmacht

The Romanian Army purchased 76 StuG III Ausf Gs from Germany in 1944. When Romania switched sides in 1944, it changed the national insignia on its AFVs to a white disc with red star. This example was recaptured by the Germans and was on a Wehrmacht train bringing armored equipment back from the front in western Czechoslovakia in the spring of 1945.

A snow-camouflaged T-34 with the enlarged "Gayka" turret of the 31st Tank Corps in Tost (Toszek), Silesia, on January 22, 1945, during the advance of the 1st Ukrainian Front. This version of the T-34 remained in production into 1944, even after the advent of the up-gunned T-34-85.

leaders were unenthusiastic about the formation of Russian units. This attitude began to change in the final months of the war, and efforts were made to begin forming Russian infantry divisions. The first infantry division had a reconnaissance battalion equipped with over a dozen Jagdpanzer 38(t)s. The Vlasov units saw some combat use in 1945, but they switched sides during the Prague uprising, supporting the Czech insurgents against the Germans.

A pair of T-34-85s of the 55th Guards Tank Regiment, 12th Guards Mechanized Brigade, 5th Guards Mechanized Corps, in February 1945 while taking part in the in the Western Carpathian offensive with the 4th Ukrainian Front.

### Red Army

During the 1944 battles, the Wehrmacht units claimed to have destroyed 32,257 Soviet tanks and AFVs; these claims were reduced to 20,150 by the Fremde Heere Ost intelligence agency due to the perennial problem of exaggerated kill claims. Actual Soviet tank and AFV losses in 1944 had been 23,700, although a significant fraction of these were due to mechanical exhaustion, accidents, and other non-combat causes. On January 1, 1945, the Red Army had a tank park of 35,400 tanks and AFVs, of which 8,300 were deployed in frontline units.

| Soviet tank and AFV strength, January 1, 1945 | |
| --- | --- |
| Heavy tanks | 4,700 |
| Medium tanks | 12,400 |
| Light tanks | 8,200 |
| *Tanks subtotal* | *25,300* |
| Heavy assault guns | 2,400 |
| Medium assault guns | 2,100 |
| Light assault guns | 5,500 |
| *Assault guns subtotal* | *10,000* |
| **Total** | **35,300** |

The principal armored formations of the Red Army were the tank corps (TK: *tankoviy korpus*) and mechanized corps (MK: *mekhanizirovanniy*

---

**D**

### 1. T-34-85, 44TH GUARDS TANK BRIGADE, 11TH GUARDS TANK CORPS, 1ST GUARDS TANK ARMY, BERLIN, APRIL 1945

The 11th Guards Tank Corps had a simple tactical symbol for its three tank brigades, consisting of small white rectangles on the front of the turret stacked above each other. One rectangle indicated the 40th, two the 44th, and three the 45th Guards Tank Brigade. The brigades also used a fairly common style of movement marking, intended to aid military police in directing traffic: a diamond split in half. The upper half included the tank brigade number, while the lower half had the individual tank number.

### 2. T-34-85, 63RD GUARDS TANK BRIGADE, 10TH GUARDS TANK CORPS, 4TH GUARDS TANK ARMY, PRAGUE, MAY 1945

The 10th Guards Tank Corps used a geometric design with vertical bars to indicate its three tank brigades: one bar for the 61st, two for the 62nd, and three for the 63rd Guards Tank Brigade. The vehicle tactical number was painted above this, the first indicating the battalion, followed by the individual tank number. Other armored units in the corps used the same insignia, minus any of the vertical bars.

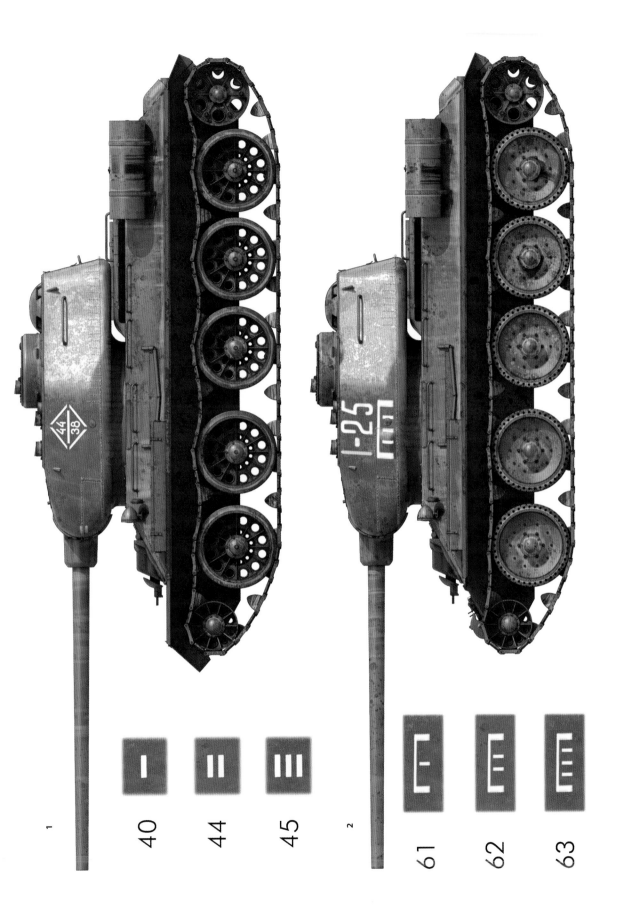

1

40

44

45

2

61

62

63

*korpus*). Although formally called corps, they were more similar in size to divisions and were renamed as such after the war. As in the case of Wehrmacht divisions, Soviet corps frequently operated well below their notional paper strength. The tank corps under the January 1945 *shtat* (table of equipment) had three tank brigades, a motor rifle brigade, and three self-propelled assault gun regiments (light, medium, and heavy). This included 207 medium tanks and 21 each of the SU-76, SU-85, and ISU-152. Many had an attached heavy tank regiment. The mechanized corps was similarly organized, but with the balance of tank/motor rifle brigades reversed, so each had three mechanized brigades and only one tank brigade. Since the mechanized brigades each had an organic tank regiment, the corps had a substantial armored force, including 183 T-34 tanks and 21 each of the SU-76, SU-85, and ISU-152. For major offensive operations, the Red Army typically organized a few tank and mechanized corps along with smaller supporting formations into a tank army (*tankoviy armiya*). In spite of the difference in nomenclature, these were comparable to a German Panzer-Korps.

The Red Army's rifle divisions had no organic armor. To provide tank support for infantry units, the Red Army deployed separate tank brigades (OTB: *otdelnaya tankovaya brigada*) and separate tank regiments (OTP: *otdelniy tankoviy polk*). The tank brigades were generally equipped with T-34 or M4A2 medium tanks, though there were smaller numbers of heavy tank brigades (TTB: *tyzhëlaya tankovaya brigada*). Tank brigades had three battalions of 21 tanks each for a total of 65 tanks per brigade, including headquarters tanks. The brigades were usually assigned to rifle corps for operations. The separate tank regiments were smaller, usually consisting of four tank companies totaling 41 tanks. These were generally assigned to support rifle divisions. As in the case of the brigades, there were specialized versions of these regiments. The best known was the Guards heavy tank breakthrough regiment (gv.TTP: *gvardeiskiy tyazhëliy tankoviy polk proryva*) that was equipped with IS-2 heavy tanks. Seven tank regiments were configured as engineer tank regiments, equipped with flamethrower tanks and mine-clearing tanks. Most belonged to the engineer assault brigades.

Self-propelled artillery was organized much like the separate tank units, with the self-propelled artillery brigade (SABr: *samokhodnaya-artilleriyskaya brigada*) and self-propelled artillery regiment (SAP: *samokhodniy-artilleriyskiy polk*). These were distinguished by the type of equipment they used, whether the light SU-76 (*leghkiy*), medium SU-85 (*sredniy*), or heavy ISU-122/ISU-152 (*tyzëliy*). As was the case with tank units, the assault gun brigades were generally deployed for corps support while the regiments were frequently doled out to rifle divisions for specific operations. Unlike the Wehrmacht, the Red Army did not make a distinction between assault gun and tank destroyer units. All were simply called self-propelled artillery (*samokhodnaya artilleriya*), even though the medium types such as the SU-85 and SU-100 were clearly oriented to the tank destroyer role.

The vehicle commanders of a battery of ISU-152 heavy assault guns consult with Senior Lieutenant Morgunov of the 1419th Heavy SP Artillery Regiment, 7th Guards Tank Corps, in Częstochowa, Poland, on January 17, 1945, during the Vistula–Oder offensive. The assault gun behind them is named "Moskva" (Moscow).

Among the allied tank units raised by the Red Army was the Yugoslav 2nd Tank Brigade, which supported the final Yugoslav partisan offensives in April 1945. This T-34-85 tank is seen in Vinkovici, Croatia, following its liberation.

The accompanying chart shows the number of the major Red Army armored formations at the beginning of January 1945. It is arranged geographically, starting with the Leningrad Front in the north. Red Army fronts were roughly comparable to US or British field armies.

| Red Army armored formations, January 1945 | | | | | | |
|---|---|---|---|---|---|---|
| Fronts | Tank Corps | Mech Corps | Tank Bde | Tank Regt | SP Arty Bde | SP Arty Regt |
| Leningrad | | | | 3 | | 1 |
| 2nd Baltic | 1 | | 1 | 2 | | 7 |
| 1st Baltic | | 1 | 4 | 5 | | 16 |
| 3rd Belorussian | 2 | | 6 | 6 | | 17 |
| 2nd Belorussian | 5 | 1 | 2 | 7 | | 22 |
| 1st Belorussian | 5 | 2 | 4 | 11 | 2 | 20 |
| 1st Ukrainian | 6 | 3 | 3 | 13 | 3 | 15 |
| 4th Ukrainian | | | 3 | 2 | | 6 |
| 2nd Ukrainian | 2 | 2 | 1 | 2 | 1 | 3 |
| 3rd Ukrainian | 3 | 1 | | 1 | | 8 |
| **Total** | **24** | **10** | **24** | **52** | **6** | **115** |

## Soviet allies

The Red Army formed several allied armies between 1943 and 1945. The largest and most significant of these was the Polish People's Army (LWP: *Ludowe Wojsko Polskie*). By 1945, this included the 1st Armored Corps (*1 Korpus Pancerny*), which was organized and equipped like a Soviet tank corps. Two heavy tank regiments were formed based on IS-2 tanks, the 4th Heavy Tank Regiment supporting the Polish 1st Army and the 5th Heavy Tank Regiment supporting the Polish 2nd Army. There were also a number of self-propelled artillery units for infantry support. The LWP took part in the January 1945 offensive, the Berlin campaign, and the final battles near Prague in May 1945. The LWP received 517 T-34 and IS-2 tanks during the war, of which 220 (62 T-34s, 132 T-34-85s, and 26 IS-2s) were still in service at the end of the war.

Nearly the entire production run of the T48 57mm gun motor carriage was sent to the Soviet Union under the Lend-Lease Program. They were known as the SU-57 in Soviet service. This example from the 70th Guards Self-propelled Artillery Brigade is seen in Prague in May 1945.

The 1st Czechoslovak Army was a symbolic political effort with very modest strength at the end of the war, since there were so few Czechoslovaks available for recruitment until well into 1945. This unit included the Czechoslovak 1st Tank Brigade, organized in Soviet fashion, which took part in the final campaign in Prague in 1945. Likewise, the Red Army formed the Yugoslav 2nd Tank Brigade in March 1945, largely as a symbolic counterbalance to the 1st Tank Brigade raised by Britain in Italy in 1944. It saw some fighting in the final weeks of the war in Yugoslavia.

Two of Germany's eastern allies, Romania and Bulgaria, switched sides in the summer of 1944. Romania's modest tank force was largely destroyed around Stalingrad in late 1942 and early 1943. Germany was reluctant to re-equip it with new tanks, though modest numbers of PzKpfw IVs and StuG IIIs were supplied prior to Romania's defection. As a result, Romania was obliged to equip itself. Its old Renault R 35 light tanks were up-gunned using 45mm tank guns from captured Soviet 1941-era tanks. Captured Soviet T-60s were rebuilt with Soviet 76mm F-22 divisional guns as the TACAM T-60 tank destroyers. Similarly, old R-2 light tanks, a Romanian variant of the PzKpfw 35(t), were rebuilt as TACAM R-2 tank destroyers with Soviet ZIS-3 76mm divisional guns. Romania developed the Mareşal light tank destroyer in 1944, which influenced the German Jagdpanzer 38(t) design. There were plans to create 32 antitank battalions, each with 30 Mareşals, but this never took place because Romania's defection in August 1944 cut off the supply of Czech engines and technical support. The Romanian 2nd Tank Regiment, with about 66 Pz Kpfw IV and R-35/45 tanks, plus 80 other armored vehicles, fought in Czechoslovakia, ending the war near Vienna. The Red Army supplied small numbers of T-34-85 tanks to the Romanian Army in the final weeks of the war, but it remained primarily equipped with armored vehicles of German origin.

**E**

### 1. IS-2, POLISH 5 PUŁK CZOŁGÓW CIĘŻKICH, 2 ARMIA WP, KODERSDORF, APRIL 1945

During the battle of Bautzen (*Budiszyn*) in Lower Silesia on April 19, 1945, 17 Panther tanks of Major Karl Rossmann's Fallschirm-Panzer-Regiment.1 ambushed the Polish 1st Tank Corps near Mückenhain and Kodersdorf, claiming to have destroyed 60 tanks. This was a significant exaggeration, as Polish AFV casualties of all types that day totaled just 44 tanks, of which many were knocked out in other sectors. This IS-2 from the 5th Heavy Tank Regiment was one of the tanks destroyed during the day's fighting. The tactical number indicates that this was the tank of the commander of 1.Kompania, with the "5" indicating the regiment and the "1" the company. It was named Tadeuz (*Theodore*) and carries the usual Piast eagle emblem of the Polish People's Army (LWP: *Ludowe Wojsko Polskie*).

### 2. IS-2, POLISH 4 PUŁK CZOŁGÓW CIĘŻKICH, 1 ARMIA WP, GERMANY, APRIL 1945

The Polish 4th Heavy Tank Regiment used a variation on the usual Piast eagle, painting it on a red diamond. In April 1945, the Allies agreed on air identification markings to avoid fratricide when the Western and Eastern Fronts converged. The Red Army selected one of its common maneuver markings, a white cross on the top of the tank turret and a white band around the turret. This was followed by some Allied units, including the Polish People's Army as seen here. On April 29, the Red Army informed the Western Allies that it had captured some German tanks with the Soviet air recognition marking. Therefore, as of May, Soviet vehicles were supposed to substitute a new marking consisting of a white triangle on the roof and a white triangle on either side of the turret. However, this new marking was not widely adopted.

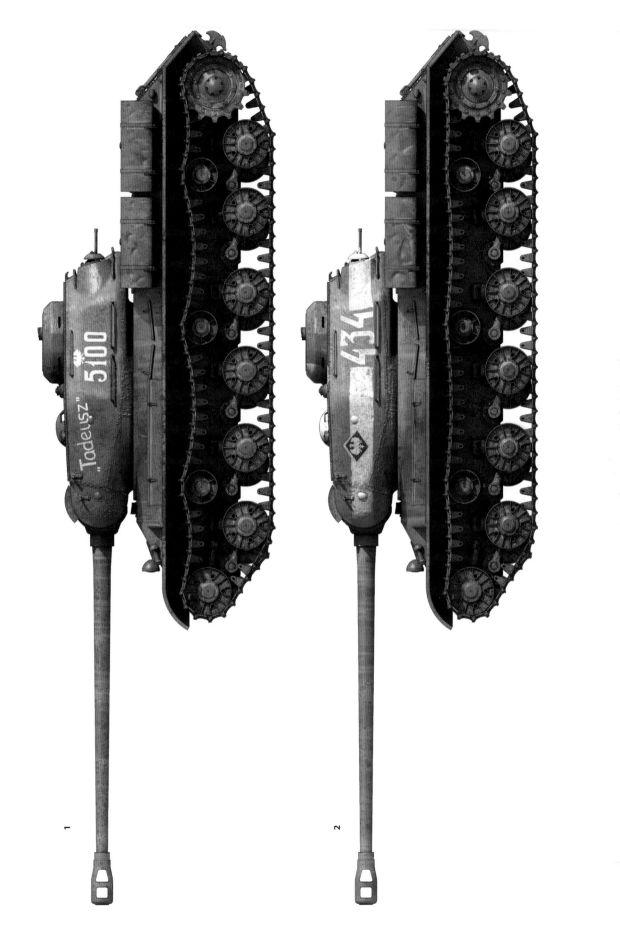

1

2

Although allied to Germany, Bulgaria took no part in the war against the Soviet Union. In July 1943, Germany supplied Bulgaria with 46 Pz Kpfw IVs, ten Pz Kpfw IIIs, and 25 StuG IIIs. Bulgaria switched sides in September 1944 when the Red Army crossed its border. The Bulgarian 1st Armored Brigade, equipped with German armored vehicles, fought alongside the Red Army in the campaigns in Hungary and Yugoslavia in 1945. Local Red Army units turned over captured German tanks to the Bulgarians, including a few Panther tanks and various types of Panzerjäger.

## TECHNICAL FACTORS

### Wehrmacht

The principal German tanks on the Russian Front in 1945 were the PzKpfw IV and Panther. The balance between the two types was similar, with the number of the newer Panthers usually exceeding that of the PzKpfw IV by a small margin. The Wehrmacht had planned to replace the PzKpfw IV with the Panther, but this never proved possible due to the higher cost of the Panther and the need to maximize Panzer production. Although not a tank in the usual sense, the Jagdpanzer IV was upgraded in August 1944 with the same 75mm gun as the Panther and redesignated as the Panzer IV/70. This was intended to serve as a surrogate tank in Panzer units, though it was also deployed in Panzerjäger and Sturmgeschütz units.

The Panther was arguably the best tank on the 1945 battlefield, with an excellent balance of firepower, armored protection, and mobility. Its frontal armor was proof against the Soviet 85mm tank gun at normal combat ranges, even when firing high-velocity armor-piercing (HVAP) projectiles with tungsten-carbide cores. In contrast, it could penetrate the frontal armor of the T-34-85 at ranges up to 2,100 meters, and even the more heavily armored IS-2 heavy tank at 600 meters. Both the Panther and T-34-85 could knock each other out in side-on engagements at ranges in excess of 3,000 meters.

It is interesting to note that Soviet tank designers felt that the Panther's 75mm gun was inferior to the 88mm gun of the Tiger I. The Soviets argued that the 88mm KwK 36 was a better-balanced gun since it fired a much more potent high-explosive round. This reflected the different tactical outlooks of the Wehrmacht and Red Army. The Wehrmacht preferred a Panther gun optimized for antitank performance, while the Red Army wanted a more versatile gun offering both good antitank and general fire support performance.

In spite of its excellent armor and firepower, the Panther suffered from mediocre reliability due to a weak final drive in the power train. This was exacerbated by poor driver training in the final months of the war and inadequate supplies of spare parts. Many Panthers were lost when they broke down during tactical situations where they could not be recovered. Although no statistics are available for Panthers in 1945, more of them were lost in the Ardennes campaign to

An old Panther Ausf D tank of Panzergrenadier-Division Brandenburg knocked out by an IS-2m of the Polish 5th Heavy Tank Regiment during the fighting near Rothenburg/Oberlausitz shortly after the Neisse River crossing on the night of April 16/17.

mechanical breakdowns and other problems than to hostile fire.

The PzKpfw IV Ausf J was still an excellent tank in 1945, even though it was inferior to the Panther in terms of firepower, protection, and mobility. Nevertheless, its firepower was still comparable to that of the T-34-85 when firing standard armor-piercing-capped ballistic-capped (APCBC) rounds. This was because its 75mm KwK 40 gun had been optimized for antitank performance, with a relatively large propellant load. The Wehrmacht had developed

more potent HVAP ammunition for this gun, but the shortage of tungsten carbide in 1945 meant that this type of ammunition was rarely available for German tanks. In contrast, the Red Army had generous supplies of HVAP. Both the PzKpfw IV Ausf J and T-34-85 could knock each other out frontally at ranges under 1,000 meters.

The Panzer IV/70 offered the same firepower as the Panther and had excellent frontal armor. However, its use of a fixed casemate instead of a turret made it less versatile when used as a surrogate tank in close-range engagements. Its superstructure side armor was only 40mm (46mm equivalent), and the stowage of ammunition behind this meant that side penetrations frequently led to catastrophic ammunition fires.

On the other hand, the Panzer IV/70 was a very potent tank destroyer if used at long ranges. In a stand-off, tank destroyer role, its virtues such as its powerful gun and strong frontal armor could be used to best advantage, while its weak side armor was less exposed than in close-range melees. It was not an especially popular vehicle with its crews because its long gun was poorly balanced and could exacerbate powertrain and suspension problems. This was especially the case with Vomag's Panzer IV/70(V), which had a lower superstructure, since the low position of the gun made it vulnerable to being embedded in the ground when moving across irregular terrain. This was less of an issue with Alkett/Nibelungenwerke's Panzer IV/70(A) as its higher superstructure reduced the probabilities of such driving mishaps.

Production of the Tiger I tank ended in August 1944, so it was deployed in declining numbers on the Russian Front due to combat attrition. It was still an excellent tank in terms of firepower and armored protection, but it

The 2nd and 3rd Belorussian Fronts continued to clear the northern flanks along the Baltic in March and April 1945. This King Tiger tank of s.Pz.Abt.505 was one of the last two of the battalion during the final fighting around Fischhausen near Pillau during the Soviet campaign to clear the East Prussian capital of Königsberg in April 1945.

**F**

## DUEL IN FESTUNG POSEN

On January 27, 1945, the 34th Guards Heavy Breakthrough Tank Regiment advanced towards the old citadel of Festung Posen (*Poznań*, Poland) on the west bank of the Warthe (*Warta*) River through the Wilda district. The lead IS-2 tank was warned by Polish civilians that the Germans had positioned a tank on the Wilda market square (*Horst Wesel Platz/Rynek Wildecki*) that covered the various streets leading into the plaza. The tank was a Panther Ausf G of Pz.-Rgt.27, 19.Panzer-Division, one of two in the city during the siege. It was attached to a special reserve Panzer force, the Begleit-Kompanie led by Hauptmann Wolfgang von Malotki, subordinated to the Festung commander's Festungsstossreserve. Malotki commanded this Panther earlier in the day's fighting but was wounded. Under a new commander, the Panther was deployed on the plaza near the Church of Mary the Queen (*Kościół pod wezwaniem Maryi Królowej*). The IS-2 tank cautiously advanced around the corner of the street, facing into the plaza, spotting the Panther as it advanced towards the intersection. At pointblank range, the Soviet tank fired first, hitting the bow joint between the glacis plate and the lower bow plate, and probably killing the driver. At least three German crewmen bailed out of the Panther, and the IS-2 fired a second round that struck the glacis plate farther to the left.

had a weak reliability record due to declining supplies of spares. German records of the period seldom distinguish between the Tiger I and Tiger II in inventory reports, so it is difficult to be precise about the relative proportions available on the Russian Front in 1945.

Production of the larger Tiger II began in January 1944. This was the heaviest tank in widespread service during the war, and had both a formidable gun and exceptionally thick armor. However, its weight caused tactical problems since many bridges in Eastern Europe could not accommodate its bulk. It was relatively uncommon on the Russian Front, with total operational strength of both Tiger types seldom more than about 125 tanks.

### Comparative tank gun technical data, 1945

| Caliber | **76mm** | **75mm** | **75mm** | **85mm** | **88mm** | **122mm** |
|---|---|---|---|---|---|---|
| Army | USSR | Germany | Germany | USSR | Germany | USSR |
| Gun type | F-34, ZIS-5 | KwK 40 | KwK 42 | ZIS-S-53 | KwK 43 | D-25 |
| Tube length | L/41.6 | L/48 | L/70 | L/52 | L/71 | L/48 |
| Armor-piercing projectile | BR-350A | Pz.Gr.39 | Pz.Gr.39/42 | BR-365 | Pz.Gr.39/43 | BR-471B |
| Type | APCBC | APCBC | APCBC | AP | APCBC | APC |
| Initial muzzle velocity (m/s) | 662 | 790 | 925 | 792 | 1,000 | 795 |
| Projectile weight (kg) | 6.3 | 6.8 | 6.8 | 9.02 | 10.2 | 25.0 |
| Penetration (mm; @500m, 30 degrees) | 59 | 91–96 | 117–129 | 90 | 185 | 122 |
| Armor-piercing projectile (high velocity) | BR-350P | Pz.Gr.40* | Pz.Gr.40/42* | BR-365P | Pz.Gr.40/43* | n/a |
| Type | HVAP | HVAP | HVAP | HVAP | HVAP | |
| Initial muzzle velocity (m/s) | 965 | 930 | 1,120 | 1,030 | 1,130 | |
| Projectile weight (kg) | 3.02 | 4.1 | 5.74 | 4.99 | 7.3 | |
| Penetration (mm; @500m, 30 degrees) | 77 | 108–120 | 174–184 | 90 | 217 | |
| High explosive projectile | O-350A | Spr.Gr.34 | Spr.Gr.42 | O-365 | Spr.Gr.43 | OF-462 |
| Projectile weight (kg) | 6.2 | 5.74 | 5.74 | 9.57 | 9.4 | 21.7 |
| Explosive fill (g) | 490 | 653 | 653 | 775 | 861 | 3,460 |

*German tungsten-carbide core ammunition rarely available in 1945.

Some of the old PzKpfw 38(t) light tanks were used as scout tanks by divisional reconnaissance battalions. This PzKpfw 38(t) Ausf C of Panzer-Aufklärungs-Abteilung.24, 12.Panzer-Division, was lost during the fighting with the Red Army on January 26, 1945, in the East Prussian town of Tolkemit.

The single most common Wehrmacht AFV on the Russian Front in 1945 was the StuG III assault gun. This formed the backbone of the Sturmgeschütz-Brigaden, supplemented by some of the less common StuG IVs on the PzKpfw IV chassis. The StuG III was originally intended for infantry support, but when Heinz Guderian became the head of the Inspector of Panzer Forces headquarters, he gradually siphoned off a portion of its production for the Panzer divisions. Some Panzer divisions received a battalion of StuG IIIs instead of a Panzerjäger battalion.

Based on the PzKpfw III chassis, the StuG III was armed with a derivative of the 75mm gun on the PzKpfw IV but in a fixed casemate instead of a turret. It was originally intended for direct, high-explosive fire support of the infantry. However, due to the threat of Soviet tanks, it was also used increasingly in an antitank role. From the start of Operation *Barbarossa* in June 1941 through August 1944, Sturmgeschütz units claimed 18,261 kills against Soviet AFVs; propaganda reports rounded this out to 20,000. Total German claims against Soviet AFVs during this period

were 100,748, so the StuG claims represented nearly a fifth (18 percent) of the total claims, which is remarkable considering that this was not its primary mission. A survey of 23 StuG III brigades on the Russian Front from December 1, 1943, to May 31, 1944, found that about 84 percent of their ammunition was expended against unarmored targets such as infantry, buildings, and vehicles, while the remaining 16 percent was fired against tanks and other armored targets.

There were no fewer than three attempts to replace the StuG III, but it remained in production until the war's end due to its low cost and excellent combat record. It cost about one-sixth the price of a Tiger I tank. The first replacement was the StuG IV, which mounted a slightly modified version of the StuG III casemate on a PzKpfw IV chassis. It entered production in November 1943 due to the high demand for more assault guns. The next "Sturmgeschütz neuer Art" (*new type*) was the SdKfz 162, also based on the PzKpfw IV chassis. This mounted the same 75mm gun on a new, simplified casemate with better frontal armor. In the event, Guderian's Panzer Inspectorate recommended production of the Jagdpanzer IV, intended for the Panzerjäger units of the Panzer force, not assault guns for the infantry. As mentioned above, it was modernized in the summer of 1944 with the Panther's longer 75mm gun, being accepted for service as the Panzer IV/70(V).

The third and most significant "*Sturmgeschütz neuer Art*" was the Jagdpanzer 38(t), unofficially called the "Hetzer" in some units. This mounted the 75mm PaK 39 in a fully enclosed casemate on a modified Czech PzKpfw 38(t) light tank chassis. This chassis was selected for the vehicle largely to exploit the production capacity of the two tank plants in the Czech lands that were not capable of manufacturing larger and heavier types. Production started in April 1944, and by 1945 it became the second most common German armored vehicle on the Russian Front after the StuG III. It was designated as a Jagdpanzer due to Guderian's influence. It was used mainly in the Panzerjäger companies of the infantry divisions as a cheap substitute for the superior StuG III. The Jagdpanzer 38(t) had good firepower for such a small vehicle. Frontal armor protection was very good, but the side armor was just 20mm, meaning it would only protect against machine-gun fire. Its elegant and sleek design hid the fact that its fighting compartment was extremely cramped and inefficient. The vehicle commander had an especially difficult task due to the poor provisions for vision devices. It was not popular in combat use, though it was clearly superior to using a towed 75mm gun.

**ABOVE LEFT**
Only two prototypes of the Maus super-heavy tank were completed. In March 1945, the Typ 205/II second prototype was driven to Wünsdorf, south of Zossen, home of the German General Staff, to serve as part of the outer ring of Berlin's defenses. In late April, after breaking down in Wünsdorf near the intersection of Zeppelinstrasse and Zerensdorfstrasse, it was blown up by its crew before ever seeing combat. The turret of the second prototype was mated to the intact hull of the first prototype before being sent to the Soviet Army tank proving ground in Kubinka, where it remains to this day.

**ABOVE RIGHT**
One of the more obscure Red Army trophies from the Berlin operation was this prototype Ardelt 88mm PaK 43/3 Waffenträger. It had served in the Panzerjäger-Abteilung.3 of the Infanterie-Division Ulrich von Hutten in Brandenburg outside Berlin in 1945. It was subsequently transported to the main proving ground at Kubinka outside Moscow.

The whole range of tank destroyers were deployed on the Russian Front, including handfuls of the old Marder types, as well as heavy 88mm tank destroyers such as the Jagdpanther and Nashorn. Both types were relatively uncommon. Surprisingly, the first Jagdtiger battalion was deployed against the US Army in western Germany rather than on the Russian Front. A few Jagdtigers did show up in the east, mainly in the final battles.

This Jagdpanzer 38(t) served in Panzerjäger-Abt.173 of the 73.Infanterie-Division. There are conflicting accounts of its destruction on January 17, 1945, during the Oder–Vistula offensive. Some reports claim that it was hit on the right side by an SU-76M, with the 76mm round detonating the ammunition inside; another version has it blown up by its own crew. It was recovered in 1989 from the Utrata River, west of Warsaw.

| German tank and AFV production, 1944–45 | | |
|---|---|---|
| | **1944** | **1945** |
| PzKpfw IV | 3,126 | 365 |
| Panther | 3,749 | 459 |
| Tiger I | 623 | |
| Tiger II | 377 | 112 |
| Panzer IV/70 | 767 | 441 |
| Marder III | 308 | |
| Nashorn | 133 | 66 |
| Jagdpanther | 226 | 166 |
| Jagdtiger | 61 | 16 |
| Jagdpanzer 38(t) | 1,457 | 1,127 |
| StuG III | 3,840 | 864 |
| StuH | 903 | 95 |
| SturmPz IV | 215 | 17 |
| StuG IV | 1,006 | 102 |
| **Total** | **16,791** | **3,830** |

G

### 1. JAGDPANZER 38(T), 25.ROHAMTÜZÉR OSZTÁLY (HUNGARIAN 25TH ASSAULT GUN BATTALION), OPERATION FRÜHLINGSERWACHEN, HUNGARY, MARCH 1945

Hungary was allotted 50 Jagdpanzer 38(t) tank destroyers from October and November 1944 orders, and they were delivered in December 1944. They were mainly used to form assault gun battalions in support of the Hungarian infantry divisions. They remained in their original Czech factory colors. The 25th Assault Gun Battalion added tactical numbers in white, as seen here, painted over the German Balkan Cross. They do not appear to have carried Hungarian national insignia. This vehicle, T-040, carried the name "Marika" on the glacis plate.

### 2. JAGDPANZER 38(T), 1600-Y OTDELNIY RAZVEDYVATELNIY DIVIZION, 1 PEKHOTNAYA DIVIZYA VS KONR, PRAGUE, MAY 1945

The Wehrmacht formed the 1st Infantry Division of the KONR (*Komitet osvobozhdeniya narodov Rossii*: Committee for the Liberation of the Russian People) in November 1944 as part of General A. A. Vlasov's ROA (*Russkaya Osvoboditelnaya Armiya*: Russian Liberation Army), which comprised Soviet prisoners of war. The performance of Major B. A. Kostenko's 1600th Separate Reconnaissance Battalion (*russische Einzel-Aufklärungs-Abt.1600*) in early 1945 led to a decision to equip it with more modern German AFVs than the old captured Soviet equipment it had been using. As a result, it received a few dozen Jagdpanzer 38(t)s. These were generally marked with "ROA" in Cyrillic on the hull sides. This particular vehicle had a three-digit tactical number, but this may have been left over from the original German unit. In the event, the Russian division switched sides during the Prague uprising in May 1945, supporting the Czech insurgents.

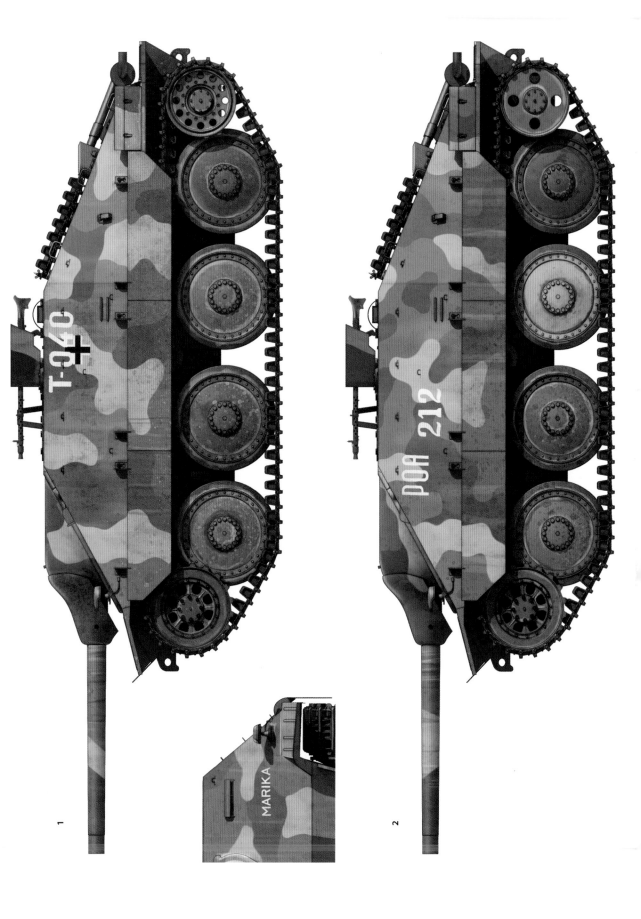

1

2

## Red Army

The backbone of the Soviet tank force was the T-34. The standard version with the 76mm Gayka hexagonal turret remained in production at four plants through March 1944. Three of the plants gradually transitioned to production of the improved T-34-85 from January 1944, while the Chelyabinsk plant shifted entirely to heavy tanks and assault guns. Production of the 76mm T-34 continued at the Omsk plant until September 1944. Total production in 1944 was 4,086 T-34s and 10,662 T-34-85s, so both types were widely deployed in the 1945 campaigns.

The T-34 Model 1944 was a modestly improved version of the tank that had been manufactured since 1941. The enlarged Gayka turret was introduced in early 1942 and can be easily distinguished by its hexagonal shape and two circular roof hatches. In 1943, the turret was improved by the addition of a cupola for the tank commander that offered better all-round vision. In terms of firepower, protection, and mobility, the T-34 Model 1944 was not significantly different than the previous production series. The most significant change was the introduction of a quality control and standardization effort in mid-1943 by the lead T-34 plant in Nizhni-Tagil. Production in 1942 and 1943 frequently focused on quantity over quality, leading to complaints from the tank troops about the high breakdown rate of the T-34. The new program was aimed at ensuring that all tanks were capable of operating for at least 300km without breakdowns. By 1944, quality control had significantly improved, along with overall T-34 reliability.

In mid-1943, the Red Army planned to replace the T-34 and KV with a new "universal tank" that was the size of a medium tank but with the armor of a heavy tank. The battle of Kursk ended this program since it revealed the need for better firepower rather than better armor. The T-34 follow-on, the T-43, was canceled in favor of mounting a more powerful 85mm gun in a new, enlarged turret. The Red Army had recognized for some time that the two-man turret as used on the T-34 was a tactical mistake since the commander was distracted by the need to load the gun as well as lead the tank. The still-born T-43 had introduced a three-man turret, and this served as the basis for the new T-34-85 turret. The initial production of the T-34-85 used the D-5 85mm gun of the SU-85 assault gun, but it was too clumsy for the modest turret volume. As a result, it was quickly replaced with the ZIS-S-53 85mm, which was better suited to use in a tank turret. Besides the enhanced firepower of the new gun, the new variant introduced the TSh-16 telescopic sight, based on captured German tank telescopic sights. A 1944 Finnish assessment of this sight noted that the telescope of the T-34-85 was "greatly superior to the sight of the T-34 Model 1942 and 1943 tanks. The clarity of the sight is on the level of the German 75mm PaK 40 anti-tank gun." This significantly improved the firepower of the T-34-85 in long-range engagements.

Overall, the T-34-85 was more comparable in size, weight, and firepower to the PzKpfw IV Ausf J than to the Panther. Although the 85mm gun was a larger caliber than the PzKpfw IV's 75mm gun, actual anti-armor performance

A column of T-34 tanks of the 5th Shock Army pass by the Hotel Astoria in Leipzig. The city was captured by the US Army and turned over to the Red Army after the war's end. The T-34s are the final production configuration with the Gayka turret with commander's cupola.

was fairly similar because the German gun used a more powerful propellant charge relative to the weight of the projectile. As mentioned previously, the T-34-85 could only penetrate the frontal armor of the Panther at very close ranges with the tungsten carbide HVAP projectile. The T-34-85 and PzKpfw IV were much more closely matched in overall firepower and armor characteristics.

The Red Army was well aware of the shortcomings of the T-34-85 compared to the Panther. However, they preferred to produce large numbers of the T-34-85 rather than shift to the production of smaller numbers of a better design. A new design, the T-44, was already available at the end of 1944. This used a completely new hull design with torsion-bar suspension and much thicker frontal armor. It was powered by the same diesel engine as the T-34-85 and used a turret derived from the T-34-85. Serial production began in January 1945. No T-44s were deployed in combat, but it is unclear if this was due to early teething problems or the desire to keep the new design secret.

The Red Army also made extensive use of the M4A2 and M4A2 (76mm) tanks in 1944 and 1945, obtained through Lend-Lease. A total of 2,345 were sent in 1944 and 814 in 1945, equivalent to about 13 percent of Soviet medium tank production in this period.

The KV heavy tank ended production in 1943. As was the case for the T-34, the battle of Kursk led to a reassessment of future requirements. The new IS-122 tank was intended as a "breakthrough" tank to provide armored firepower for infantry assaults. It offered sufficient frontal protection when faced by the ubiquitous 75mm PaK 40. Although consideration was given to arming it with the new D-10 100mm gun, the Red Army eventually settled on using the D-25 122mm version, which was selected due to its powerful high-explosive firepower, not its anti-armor performance. It also benefited from an existing supply network for the 122mm ammunition, which the 100mm gun did not enjoy. The main problem with the IS-122 was that the large size of the two-piece ammunition and the limited internal volume of the tank meant that it carried only 28 rounds of ammunition. The IS-122 was deployed in heavy breakthrough tank regiments subordinated to corps for offensive operations. The IS-122 was much closer in weight and other features to the Panther or Tiger I than to the Tiger II. Later, the IS-122 was referred to more simply as the IS-2, and that is the designation used elsewhere in this book. A follow-on design, the IS-3, entered production shortly before the end of the war but was not yet ready for combat deployment.

After the war, the Soviet Army made an assessment of the relative combat effectiveness of various wartime tanks. Using the T-34 as the baseline, the other tanks were judged and AFVs were valued relative to it. T-34-85 was 1.14 times more effective than T-34.

An M4A2 (76mm) of the 8th Mechanized Corps knocked out in January 1945 during the 2nd Belorussian Front's offensive into East Prussia.

This is an early production IS-2 with the early-style narrow cast hull front manufactured in February 1944. It is currently on display at the American Heritage Museum in Stow, Massachusetts.

| Comparative combat value of Soviet AFVs, 1944–45 | | | | | |
|---|---|---|---|---|---|
| SU-76M | T-34 | T-34-85 | T-44 | IS-2 | IS-3 |
| 0.74 | 1.0 | 1.14 | 1.71 | 1.62 | 1.92 |

The second most common Soviet AFV after the T-34 was the SU-76M assault gun. As was the case with the German Jagdpanzer 38(t), this design was selected in order to exploit the limited production capacities of existing light tank plants. In the Soviet case, the SU-76M was built at plants formerly assigned to the T-70 and short-lived T-80 light tanks. This was the reason that the USSR still sought the British Valentine tank through Lend-Lease into 1944 since it could perform the light reconnaissance tank function alongside surviving T-70 light tanks. The configuration of the SU-76M was very simple, more reminiscent of the German Marder tank destroyer than the Jagdpanzer 38(t). The fighting compartment was located at the rear of the vehicle, with very modest armor protection in order to keep down weight. The SU-76M was armed with the 76mm ZIS-3 gun, the Red Army's standard divisional field gun. Although this is sometimes erroneously described as an antitank gun, it performed the same role in the Red Army as the US 105mm howitzer, British 25-pdr, or German 105mm howitzer; the antitank version of this gun was the 57mm ZIS-2. The SU-76M was used in light assault gun regiments subordinated to corps and to support rifle divisions during operations.

The other light assault gun in Red Army use was the SU-57, the Soviet designation for the US T48 57mm gun motor carriage. This was a tank-destroyer armed with the 57mm antitank gun, mounted on an M3 halftrack. The Red Army formed them into special independent tank destroyer brigades, with three battalions and 60 SU-57s each. They first saw combat during the Dnepr River offensive in Ukraine in August 1943.

The medium assault guns were based on the T-34 chassis. The SU-122 was no longer in production in 1944 and 1945, but surviving vehicles were still in use in dwindling numbers. The most common medium assault gun was the SU-85, armed with the 85mm D-5S gun. The primary role of the SU-85 was as a tank destroyer. By 1944, its firepower was inadequate to deal with threats such as the Panther, so it was upgraded into the SU-100 with the new D-10S 100mm gun. This was the most powerful antitank gun in use on Soviet AFVs during the war, and roughly comparable in performance to the German 88mm KwK 36.

The heavy assault guns were based on the IS tank chassis. These came in two principal variants: the ISU-122, armed with the A-19 122mm gun, and the ISU-152, with the ML-20S gun-howitzer. A small number of ISU-122S were built that used the D-25S 122mm gun derived from the weapon of the IS-2 tank. The reason for the use of the two different calibers of weapons was primarily due to the supply of gun barrels and ammunition rather than to different tactical requirements. Although sometimes dubbed "Zveroboi" (*Animal hunter*) for their effectiveness against the German "Cats" such as the Panther and Tiger, their primary role was direct fire support, not tank fighting.

| Soviet tank & AFV production, 1944–45 | | |
|---|---|---|
| | **1944** | **1945*** |
| T-34 | 4,086 | |
| T-34-85 | 10,662 | 9,510 |
| T-44 | 25 | 545 |
| IS | 2,250 | 2,015 |
| SU-76 | 7,155 | 2,966 |
| SU-85 | 315 | |
| SU-100 | 500 | 1,060 |
| ISU-122 | 1,170 | 740 |
| ISU-152 | 1,340 | 510 |
| **Total** | **27,503** | **17,346** |

*to September 1945

| Comparative technical characteristics | | | | |
|---|---|---|---|---|
| | **T-34-85** | **Panther Ausf G** | **IS-2** | **Tiger II** |
| Crew | **5** | **5** | **4** | **5** |
| Dimensions (L x W x H [m]) | 8.1x3.0x2.7 | 8.86x3.42x2.98 | 9.8x3.1x2.73 | 10.3x3.7x3.1 |
| Loaded weight (tonnes) | 32.2 | 45.5 | 46 | 69.8 |
| Main gun | 85mm ZIS-S-53 | 75mm KwK 42 | 122mm D-25T | 88mm KwK 43 |
| Main gun rounds | 60 | 81 | 28 | 84 |
| Engine (hp) | 500 | 600 | 520 | 600 |
| Max speed (km/h) | 55 | 46 | 37 | 41 |
| Fuel (liters) | 815 | 720 | 820 | 860 |
| Range (km) | 300 | 200 | 150 | 170 |
| Ground pressure (kg/cm2) | .83 | .88 | .81 | 1.02 |
| **Armor*** | | | | |
| Mantlet (mm) | 90*=>90 | 110*=>110 | 105*=>105 | 100*=>100 |
| Turret front (mm) | 90*=>90 | 100@11=102 | 105*=>105 | 180@10=183 |
| Turret side (mm) | 45@5=45 | 45@25=50 | 95@12=97 | 80@20=85 |
| Upper hull front (mm) | 45@60=90 | 80@55=140 | 120@65=132 | 150@50=233 |
| Lower hull front (mm) | 45@60=90 | 60@55=105 | 100@35=122 | 120@50=186 |
| Upper hull side (mm) | 45@53=73 | 50@30=58 | 95@12=97 | 80@25=88 |

*Curved

**Armor data provided as: actual thickness in mm @ angle from vertical = effective thickness in mm

| Soviet AFV deployment at war's end* | | | | | |
|---|---|---|---|---|---|
| | Front | Reserve | Military districts | Rebuilding plants | Total |
| Unidentified | 0 | 0 | 43 | 256 | 299 |
| T-26 | 35 | 0 | 213 | 176 | 424 |
| Other types | 265 | 269 | 1,750 | 676 | 2,960 |
| Lend-Lease light tanks | 207 | 109 | 295 | 303 | 914 |
| T-34 + IS | 5,640 | 963 | 1,677 | 2,032 | 10,312 |
| Lend-Lease med tanks | 877 | 219 | 275 | 446 | 1,817 |
| *Tanks subtotal* | *7,024* | *1,560* | *4,253* | *3,889* | *16,726* |
| SU-57 | 250 | 66 | 10 | 14 | 340 |
| SU-76 | 3,546 | 999 | 688 | 670 | 5,903 |
| ISU-122/-152 | 1,196 | 340 | 129 | 336 | 2,001 |
| *SU subtotal* | *4,992* | *1,405* | *827* | *1,020* | *8,244* |
| **Total AFVs** | **12,016** | **2,965** | **5,080** | **4,909** | **24,970** |

*Does not include holdings of Far Eastern or Baikal Fronts

# BATTLE ANALYSIS

The relative combat effectiveness of the German and Soviet tank forces was dominated by the numerical balance of both sides. The Soviet Union substantially outproduced Germany in tanks, further reinforced by Lend-Lease shipments from the United States. In January 1945, the Red Army had a tank and AFV inventory three times larger than Germany's: 35,400 versus 12,336. The Wehrmacht's inventory on the Russian Front was only a portion of the overall total, since a significant fraction of German tank strength was deployed on other fronts. In January 1945, about 40 percent of the German inventory was committed to the Russian Front; this fraction varied through time. The portion assigned to the Russian Front increased later in 1945, but it was a larger portion of a shrinking inventory due to combat attrition and the collapse of the German Panzer industry in early 1945. As a result, the Panzer force was generally confronted by substantially more numerous opponents.

The Wehrmacht's other underlying problem was the collapse of its fuel supply due to the Allied Oil Campaign against the German fuel industry that had started in May 1944.[2] General Alfred Jodl, chief of staff of the OKH (Army High Command), later stated that the main reason the Wehrmacht was unable to use its large Panzer reserve to repulse the Soviet Vistula–Oder offensive in January 1945 was severe fuel shortages that kept portions of the Panzer reserve immobile.

The fuel shortage had other deleterious effects on the combat effectiveness of the Panzer force in 1945, also severely curtailing Wehrmacht Panzer driver training and small unit tactical training.

At the tactical level, from 1941–44 the Wehrmacht had managed to fight the Red Army while outnumbered and often emerge victorious. However, by 1945, the tactical and technical prowess of the Wehrmacht over the Red Army had substantially declined. Red Army training in 1944 and 1945 was better than in 1942 and 1943, and the Soviet tank industry had paid greater attention to improving the overall reliability of new tanks.

A battery of SU-100s of the 1893rd Self-Propelled Artillery Regiment, 6th Guards Tank Corps, in the Prague suburbs in May 1945 after the liberation of the Czech capital.

2  Steven Zaloga, *The Oil Campaign 1944–45*, Osprey Air Campaign (2022).

| Soviet tank and AFV losses in 1945 by campaign | | |
|---|---|---|
| Campaign | Total losses | Avg daily loss |
| Budapest offensive, Oct 29, 1944 to Feb 13, 1945 | 1,766 | 16 |
| Vistula–Oder offensive, Jan 12 to Mar 2, 1945 | 1,267 | 55 |
| Western Carpathian offensive, Jan 12 to Feb 18, 1945 | 359 | 9 |
| East Prussian offensive, Jan 13 to Apr 25, 1945 | 3,525 | 34 |
| Eastern Pomeranian offensive, Feb 10 to Apr 4, 1945 | 1,027 | 19 |
| Vienna offensive, Mar 16 to May 8, 1945 | 603 | 19 |
| Berlin offensive, Apr 16 to May 8, 1945 | 1,997 | 87 |
| Prague offensive, May 6–May 11, 1945 | 373 | 62 |
| *Subtotal AFV losses during listed campaigns* | *10,917* | |
| **Total tank losses in 1945** | **8,700** | |
| **Total SU losses in 1945** | **5,000** | |
| **Total AFV losses in 1945** | **13,700** | **105** |

# TECHNICAL LESSONS

The postwar Soviet Army conducted extensive studies of wartime tank fighting to help determine future tank design and tactics. This operational research provides some interesting information on various technical aspects of tank combat in 1945. Data on German experiences in 1945 is generally lacking, in part because the Wehrmacht did not show as much interest in operational research as did the Red Army, but also due to the chaos and confusion of the final months of the war.

Soviet postwar studies concluded that enemy gunfire was the predominant cause of tank and AFV casualties during the 1945 fighting. There is no breakdown of the relative percentage of AFV guns versus towed antitank guns, since battlefield research could determine the caliber but not the source of the enemy gunfire.

A column of ISU-122 heavy assault guns on the streets of Berlin following the conclusion of the battle for the German capital.

| Soviet tank and assault gun casualties by cause, February–March 1945 | | | | | | | | | |
|---|---|---|---|---|---|---|---|---|---|
|  | Gunfire | Mines | Aircraft | RPG | Drowning | Swamps | Ditches | Technical | Total |
| February (no.) | 4,286 | 295 | 125 | n/a | 21 | 370 | 60 | 604 | **5,761** |
| February (%) | 74.2 | 5.1 | 2.2 | n/a | 0.4 | 6.4 | 1.2 | 10.5 | |
| March (no.) | 4,994 | 281 | 42 | 181 | 47 | 658 | 90 | 799 | **7,092** |
| March (%) | 71 | 4 | 0.6 | 2.5 | 0.6 | 9.1 | 1.2 | 11 | |

The Soviet investigations concluded that German 75mm and 88mm guns were the predominant cause of Soviet tank and AFV battlefield casualties in 1945. Some of the outliers were casualties to German 105mm and 128mm Flak guns, as well as those to outdated 37mm and 50mm guns during the last-ditch battles in Berlin in April and May 1945.

| Combat losses of the T-34 Tank by German weapon caliber in 1945 (percent) | | | | | | | | |
|---|---|---|---|---|---|---|---|---|
|  | 37mm | 50mm | 75mm | 88mm | 105mm | 128mm | RPG | Unknown |
| 1st Belorussian Front, Jan–Mar 1945 | | | 29.0 | 64.0 | | 1.0 | 5.5 | 0.5 |
| 1st Ukrainian Front, Mar 1945 | | 0.5 | 19.0 | 71.0 | 0.6 | | 8.9 | |
| 4th Ukrainian Front, May 1945 | | | 25.3 | 51.5 | 0.9 | | 9.0 | 13.3 |
| 1st Belorussian Front, Oder–Berlin 1945 | | 1.4 | 69.2 | 16.7 | | | 10.5 | 2.2 |
| 2nd Guards Tank Army, Berlin operation 1945 | 5.4 | | 36.0 | 29.0 | 6.6 | | 22.8 | |

Tank combat on the Russian Front in 1945 generally took place at longer ranges than in the West due to the topography. Poland in particular has especially flat terrain. The accompanying chart shows the average ranges at which Soviet tanks were hit by the predominant German AFV weapons, the 75mm and 88mm guns.

| Soviet tank and assault gun casualties by range in 1945 (percent) | | |
|---|---|---|
| Distance (m) | 75mm gun | 88mm gun |
| 100–200 | 10.0 | 4.0 |
| 200–400 | 26.1 | 14.0 |
| 400–600 | 33.3 | 18.0 |
| 600–800 | 14.5 | 31.2 |
| 800–1,000 | 7.0 | 13.5 |
| 1,000–1,200 | 4.5 | 8.5 |
| 1,200–1,400 | 3.6 | 7.6 |
| 1,400–1,600 | 0.4 | 2.0 |
| 1,600–1,800 | 0.4 | 0.7 |
| 1,800–2,000 | - | 0.3 |

# FURTHER READING

The history of tank combat on the Russian Front in 1945 has enjoyed a literary renaissance in recent years, with particularly good new coverage of the fighting in Hungary and Berlin. There have also been some notable English translations of recent Russian works, such as Nebolsin's histories of the Guards tank armies, and Harrison's translations of the Soviet General Staff studies. Statistical data on the Red Army in this book has come from various published Russian accounts as well as Polonskiy's collection of Soviet armored force records cited below. The German statistical data comes primarily from the records of the Inspector General of Panzer Forces, found in the T-78 collection of OKH records in Record Group 242 Captured German Records at the US National Archives and Records Administration in College Park, Maryland.

The bibliography here focuses on campaign histories. There are many specialized monographs on the various types of tanks and AFVs covered in this book, but they are too numerous to list here.

An IS-2 tank of the 7th Guards Breakthrough Heavy Tank Regiment of the 2nd Belorussian Front in front of the Brandenburg Gate in Berlin at the end of the fighting. The tank has the Allied recognition band around the turret along with the regimental insignia, a stalking bear on a red star.

Archer, Lee, *et al.*, *Panzers in Berlin 1945*, Panzerwrecks, Old Heathfield (2019).

Harrison, Richard (ed.), *Prelude to Berlin: The Red Army's Offensive Operations in Poland and Eastern Germany 1945: Soviet General Staff Studies*, Helion, Solihull (2016).

Harrison, Richard (ed.), *The Berlin Operation: Soviet General Staff Studies*, Helion, Solihull (2016).

Isaev, Aleksei & Kolomiets, Maksim, *Tomb of the Panzerwaffe: The defeat of the Sixth SS Panzer Army in Hungary 1945*, Helion, Solihull (2014).

Jakl, Tomáš, *Prahou pod pancířem povstalců*, Mladá Front, Prague (2010).

Jakl, Tomáš, *Prahou pod pancířem vlasovců*, Mladá Front, Prague (2014).

Karalus, Maciej & Jerzak, Jarosław, *Panzers in the Defence of Festung Posen 1945*, Helion, Solihull (2018).

Krivosheyev, G. F. (ed.), *Rossiya i SSSR v voynakh XX veka: Kniga poter*, Veche, Moscow (2010).

Müller-Hillebrand, Hermann Burkardt, *Der Zweifrontkrieg: Das Heer vom Beginn des Feldzuges die Sowjetunion bis zum Kriegsende, Band III*, E. S. Mittler & Sohn, Frankfurt (1969).

Nash, Douglas, *From the Realm of a Dying Sun. Volume III: IV. SS-Panzerkorps from Budapest to Vienna, February–May 1945*, Casemate, Havertown (2021).

Nebolsin, Igor, *Pervaya iz gvardeyskikh 1-ya gv. Tankovaya armiya v boyu*, Yauza, Moscow (2016).

Nebolsin, Igor, *Stalin's Favorite: The Combat History of the 2nd Guards Tank Army from Kursk to Berlin, Vol. 2*, Helion, Solihull (2015).

Nebolsin, Igor, *Tank Battles in East Prussia and Poland 1944–1945*, Helion, Solihull (2019).

Nevenkin, Kamen, *Bloody Vienna: The Soviet Offensive Operations in Western Hungary and Austria, March–May 1945*, PeKo, Keszthely (2020).

Polonskiy, V. A., (ed.) *Glavnoe avtobronetankovoe upravlenie: Lyudi, cobytiya, fakty v dokumentakh, Vol. 5*, Russian Defense Ministry, Moscow (2005).

Schäufler, Hans, *1945 – Panzer an der Weichsel, Soldaten der letzen Stunde*, Motorbuch, Stuttgart (1979).

Shein, Dmitriy, *Tanki vedet Rybalko: Boevoy put 3-y gv. tankovvoy armii*, Yauza, Moscow (2007).

Számvéber, Norbert, *Days of Battle: Armored Operations north of the River Danube, Hungary 1944–45*, Helion, Solihull (2013).

Zaloga, Steven & Ness, Leland, *Red Army Handbook 1939–1945*, Sutton, Stroud (1998).

n.a., *Boevoy sostav sovetskoy armii, jan.-avg., 1945 g.*, Voenizdat, Moscow (1990).

# INDEX

Note: Page numbers in **bold** refer to illustrations with some caption locators in brackets. Page numbers in *italic* refer to tables.